CAST ASIDE THE SHADOWS

Violet Elmer and the Carlton Works
Copeland Street, Stoke-on-Trent

Barry & Elaine Girling

Best Wishes
Barry & Elaine

This book is dedicated to the memory
of Elizabeth Jane
5.9.1969 – 6.6.2001

2012

First Edition

Published and Printed by

Leiston Press
Masterlord Industrial Estate
Leiston
Suffolk
IP16 4JD
Telephone Number: 01728 833003
Email: glenn@leistonpress.com

ISBN 978-1-907938-30-6

©Barry & Elaine Girling

All rights reserved. No part of this book may be reproduced, stored in a retrieval system, or transmitted in any form or by any means electronic, mechanical, photocopying, recording or otherwise, without the prior permission of the authors.

Contents

Contents i
Acknowledgements ii
Preface iii

Chapter 1 Miss Elmer 1
The early years – Violet and Ruby – Artistry – The move to Carlton Ware

Chapter 2 The Pottery 19
A brief history – Lifestyle – What is in a name – The premises – Kilns – Workforce, Sales and new designs – Public utilities

Chapter 3 Products 1890-1938 47
A broad overview

Chapter 4 Horace Wain Designer 1911-c.1921 51
Chinoiserie and Armand

Chapter 5 Social and Economic 53
Jazz age – General strike – Wall Street and the Recession

Chapter 6 Enoch Boulton Designer c.1922-1929 55
Grimwades – Tutankhamen, Chinaland and fantasy birds – S. Fielding and Company

Chapter 7 The Art Deco Years 59
Paris Exhibition – Cinema – North America

Chapter 8 Carlton China Tea Ware 63
Birks Rawlins – Designs – Product range

Chapter 9 Handcraft 71
Influence and development

Chapter 10 Carlton Ware and Crown Devon 75
Similarity, Rivalry and The Jazz pattern

Chapter 11 Violet Elmer Designer 1928-1938 77
Change of environment – Lodgings – Floral embossed, the Influence of Violet Elmer – Wedding of Ruby Moss - Introduction to Art Deco and Best Ware – Identification of Violet Elmer's work

Chapter 12 Olive Kew Designer 1930-1931 95

Chapter 13 Irene Pemberton Designer 1938-1949 99

Chapter 14 Christopher Boulton Designer c.1952-1954 101

Chapter 15 Best Ware Designs 1930-1938 103

Chapter 16 Marriage and the Changing Times 121

Chapter 17 Products 1939-1967 123
A broad overview

Chapter 18 Technique and Decoration 129
Manufacture of a Best Ware vase – Handcraft and Best Ware shapes – Borders, friezes, finials and mounts

Chapter 19 Tributes and Obituaries 143
Christopher Boulton 1912-1978. Rose Colclough 1917- present. Olive Kew 1902 -1991. Irene Pemberton 1911-2008

Chapter 20 Mrs Violet Lawton 151

Appendices 157
a   Some prominent Violet Elmer Designs
b   Designers and modellers associated with Carlton Ware
c   Known employees pre 1939
d   Additional employees 1939-1967
e   Employees 1960 - supplementary list
f   Elmer family tree
g   Descendants of James Robinson

Selected Bibliography 169

Index 170

Acknowledgements

A debt of gratitude is owed to Harvey Pettit for valued assistance and the benefit of his research. In addition, we fully recognize his willingness to make available the details of his interviews with Olive Kew, as well as the obituary to Irene Pemberton: see www.carltonwareworld.com. We express our grateful thanks for the help received from both Helen Martin and Keith Martin, researchers and directors [Carlton Ware Collectors International Club and editors of the Carlton Times 1994 – 2001].

We appreciate the generous assistance given by: Mrs Janice Bebbington – research, John Franklin – photographs, Ian Harwood and Jerome Wilson – research and photographs, see Carlton Ware newsletters by reference to www.nicholnack.com.au [also www.carltonwareworld.com], Jane and Martin Hedger – photographs, Liz Minister – proof reader, the late John Parks – original art work, Mr E. G. Richards – private family history [Olive Kew], Colin Russell – factual information and photographs [Ruby and Violet], and Garry Strachan – research.

We gladly acknowledge the following, whose work has influenced our thinking: Pita Gregory and Jules Smith, [Carlton Ware Collectors International and the Carlton Times 1993-94], Jim King, Arthur Puffett, and Jane and Derek Towns at www.carltonchina.info.com

Additional thanks is owed The Lexi James Collection, The Dulcie Agnes Joyce Memorial Collection and The Parnell Collection for use of photographs via the kind assistance of Bruce Nichol [www.nicholnack.com.au]

We wish to register the courteous and professional support received from Companies House Cardiff, English Heritage [NMR] RAF Photography, Leiston Press Suffolk, Ordnance Survey Southampton, Oxfordshire County Council Record Office, Oxfordshire Family History Society, Oxfordshire Studies Westgate Oxford, City Archives Stoke-on-Trent, The Sentinel Newspaper, Stoke-on-Trent and the office of the Registrar at Cheshire,

Oxfordshire and Staffordshire.

Finally we are pleased to record the contribution made by: Steven Birks www.thepotteries.org, Patricia Cockerill, Alison Ginevra Durrant, Rosemary Endacott, David Forgan, John and Elizabeth Griffiths, Rose Hampson, Brenda Horwood, Nicholas Howell, Sheila Ikin, Ipswich Borough Council [The Regent Theatre], Ray Johnson, Lema Publishing [The Pottery Gazette and Glass Trade Review], Digby Martin, Graham Meredith, Mike Moore, Bob and Patricia Moss, Hilary Newberry, Carole Newbigging, Michael Perry, Mrs Audrey Plant, Liz Plant, Matthew James Plummer, Reeman Dansie, Norman Timms, Mrs Joan Whieldon [née Bamford], Liz Woolley, and to all those not mentioned by name, who helped to show us the way.

Note: In view of the paucity of information available, the authors regret any errors and omissions which may have occurred. Notwithstanding, every effort has been made, in good faith, to achieve the most accurate presentation. If this work does no more than stimulate debate or results in the acquisition of further information, it will have served its purpose. Neither the authors nor the publisher will be held responsible for any unintentional misrepresentation, or losses incurred as a consequence of the contents of this book. The authors will be pleased to receive any additional material via the publisher's address.

Preface

It was many years ago, in good company, that we stumbled across a glorious remnant of a bygone age. Little did we know that finding the long lost Post Office and china shop at Badingham, near the market town of Framlingham in Suffolk, would mark the beginning of an all consuming interest in Carlton Ware. Intrigued, we soon found ourselves within the confines of the time-worn premises.

Badingham, Suffolk

Amongst the display of china horses looking for a fresh stable, numerous dinner services salivating a first roast and novelty ware awaiting an early smile, was a pile of rouge leaf dishes proclaiming themselves to be Carlton Ware. Impressed with our friends' knowledge, we made our first purchase and thus marked a watershed in our lives.

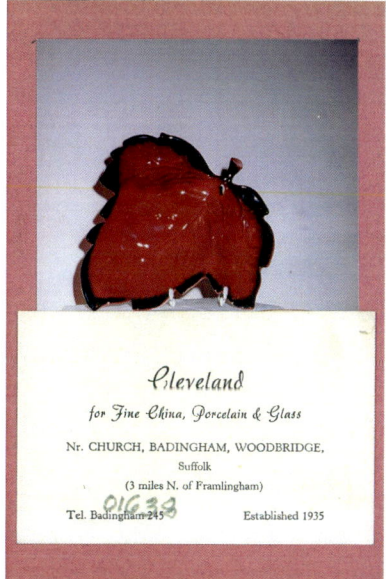

Gradually familiarising ourselves with the vast array of items produced by the Stoke-on-Trent pottery and assimilating such written knowledge as was available, our collecting habit continued. A developing attraction to the Handcraft and Best Ware products of the late 1920s and 30s was undeniable and this became our focus.

Many of the vases, ginger jars and chargers produced during this period, were designed by Violet Elmer, an artist about whom little appeared to be known. A surprising fact in view of the vast contribution that she made to the British decorative arts.

This is not only her story but that of those who were instrumental in her success.

The authors have had work on the subject of Violet Elmer and Wiltshaw and Robinson's pottery published in journals, magazines and newsletters.

The preface will not be complete without further mention of Badingham as the former home of children's book illustrators, twins, Janet and Anne Grahame Johnstone. An example of their prolific output can be found in the book "Peter Pan and Wendy" by J.M. Barrie.

Chapter 1

Miss Elmer

The early years
A distinctive late Victorian suburb of Oxford is to be found south of the river Thames [Isis] at its crossing with Folly Bridge and west of Abingdon Road. Hibbert's Encyclopaedia of Oxford records that Grandpont took its name from a causeway that once stood in this area and consisted of a series of stone bridges across the low lying

Abingdon Road looking south from Folly Bridge c.1900

lands and river. The more extensive development of this area and the subsequent estate, was stimulated by the coming of the railway in the mid century.

Built c.1893, one particular street would become the location of a meaningful event, not only for the first occupants of the newly built houses but also the wider world.

Grandpont was the birthplace of Violet Elmer, one of the foremost English designers of ceramics who has remained a little known figure. Better known contemporaries are Clarice Cliff, Susie Cooper and Charlotte Rhead. In view of the considerable body of work undertaken by Violet during the period 1928-1938, it is perhaps appropriate that, some hundred years after her birth, an assessment of her life and achievements should be made.

Edith Road, Grandpont c.1900

Violet Elmer, born Edith Road Grandpont, was the youngest of Thomas Henry and Jane Elmer's three surviving children. Her fellow siblings were Wilfred Henry George, [b.1896] Florence Esmé Nichols [b.1894] and first-born Jane [b.1891]. There must have been concern in the family when Wilfred, a journalist, found himself fighting with the British Expeditionary Force in France during 1917. Papers survive but were damaged in the Second World War. They have been trimmed by the conservers and are known as 'The Burnt Collection'.

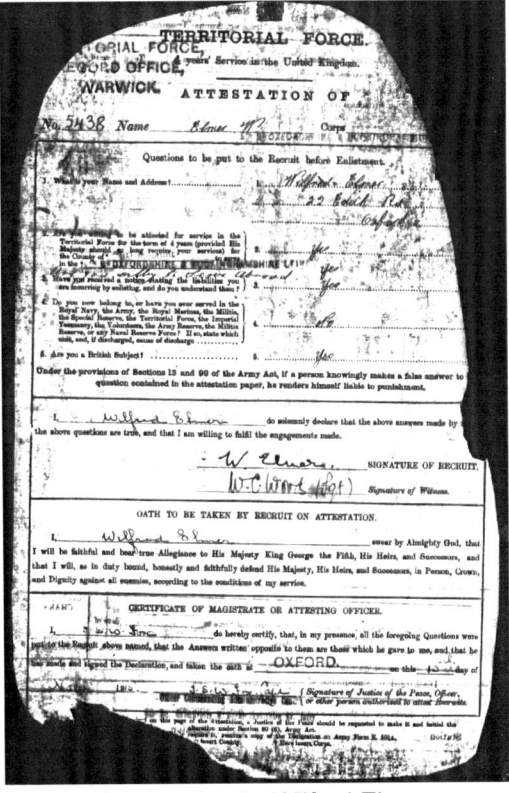

Service detail - Wilfred Elmer

Fortunately, he returned safely, to subsequently enjoy a settled married life with his wife Dorothy, née Paxford and their daughter Mary. Eldest sibling Florence did not marry and spent her early years in a business environment. At the age of seventeen she was apprenticed to learn typing and shorthand. She devoted the latter part of her life to the care of her mother. Violet's mother, Jane née Hyatt, about whom little is known, was born at Wallingford in 1868, to Henry and Ann Hyatt. Jane's brothers and sisters were Elizabeth, Dan and Mary. Sister Martha died during her first year. Of Violet Elmer's maternal grandparents, Henry [b.1838], Warborough, was a maltster and Ann [b.1842] in the nearby village of Dorchester was described as a needlewoman.

Stoke-by-Nayland, Suffolk

Stoke-by-Nayland in Suffolk, containing the great landmark church and characterised by fine buildings of the silk industry was a favourite of the painter John Constable. The village, which was the source of the male Elmer line, was the starting point of a romantic journey to Oxfordshire. The surname Elmer is local to the area and can be found predominantly in the county of Suffolk. In the 18th

St Mary's Church, Stoke-by-Nayland

century, Thomas Elmer [b.1791] and skilled in the way of the land, was living at Scotland Street with his wife Ann née Chisnell [b.1790], whom he married 25th October 1816. Also living at home, as recorded by the Census Return of 1841, were their two son's Ephraim [b.1822] and George [b.1824], similarly described as agricultural labourers. The remaining siblings Sarah [b.1817], Thomas [b.1820] and possibly George's twin sister Maria [b.1824] are unaccounted for in 1841. Although not a traveller in the spirit of St. Botolph of nearby Icanho, it was Violet's grandfather George, who was instrumental in the family move to Oxfordshire.

By 1851 George Elmer was to be found in the employ of Henry William Dashwood, Manor House, Duns Tew, Oxfordshire. George was described as "27, Servant, Groom, b. Suffolk, Stoke". It is supposition, but no less interesting, to hypothesize about how George found his

Manor House, Duns Tew
(Courtesy Oxfordshire County Council photographic archive)

way to Duns Tew, sometime between 1841 and 1851.

It is quite possible that the Elmers were originally employed locally within the large Tendring Hall Estate as well as maybe occupying one of the Estate properties. The Hall itself was demolished in 1955. As the owners, the Rowley family were related by marriage to the Dashwood family, it may be that, through this connection, George was told of the vacancy in Oxfordshire and made the move to better himself. Another theory exists, relating to Wherstead Park on the banks of the River Orwell near Ipswich. This estate, a dozen miles from Stoke-by-Nayland, was also owned at the time by a branch of the Dashwood family. There is also mention of the premier Dashwood seat of Kirtlington Park in their family memorial. From which estate George transferred will probably never be known. Violet's grandfather was still at Duns Tew in 1861 and had been promoted, in that he was described as "Servant, unmarried, aged 36, Coachman, born Suffolk, Stoke".

Wherstead Park

In 1862, George married local Oxfordshire girl Ellen Nichols [b.1842], and the link from Suffolk was made. Ellen was considerably younger than George and the daughter of Master Tailor Caleb and his wife Hannah. Caleb, the employer of two men in his tailoring business, was born at Duns Tew in 1817 whilst his wife entered the world at Kirtlington in 1816. Perhaps it is too fanciful to imagine that George and Ellen met whilst George was being fitted with his liveried uniform. It is intriguing to note that of their six children, four, namely, Mary, Frederick, Annie as well as Violet's father Thomas Henry, were all born at Kirtlington. Regarding the other two children, Barton in 1871, was the birthplace for Esme, whilst Oxford, 1875 was entrusted with Archibald's arrival. However, Kirtlington, as an address, does not feature in either the 1861 or 1871 Census.

Henry William Dashwood was an important Oxfordshire figure and a gentleman of some standing. In house at Duns Tew, eleven servants were employed ranging from governess to footman. Perhaps significantly, three of the staff emanated from Suffolk. George's employer succeeded to the title of 5th Baronet in 1861 and as Sir Henry William Dashwood Bt. may well have taken up residence at the main titled seat of the splendid palladian mansion, Kirtlington Park [built 1742-1746]. Again it is conjecture but it is possible that the coachman followed his master to the principal family estate.

Kirtlington Park (Courtesy Oxfordshire County Council photographic archive)

As time went by, George, still described as a coachman, was recorded as living with Ellen and four of their children at North Street, Steeple Barton, Woodstock in 1871. It would appear that they were living next door to Ellen's parents. It also seems that life had improved for the Elmers, as they now employed a servant, as listed at the premises was one "Susan Smith, aged 14, domestic", born nearby at Kidlington.

A decade later, the family had moved again as in 1881 the two adults and four children were listed at Albert Street Oxford. George now aged 57 was described as a mail driver and Thomas Henry aged 14, as telegraph messenger. The family did not believe in staying at any one address for very long which was proven in 1891 as Isis Street Oxford was the latest abode. George, now verging on retirement, had resorted to life as a stableman whilst his son had been elevated to postman. Although living with Jane, whom he married in 1891, and the rest of the family in Isis Street, Violet's father Thomas and his wife would leave home during the next few years. Thomas Henry was now making his own way in life within the postal service. Together with his wife, and children Florence and Wilfred, he had, by 1901, moved to a recently built property in Edith Road Oxford.

Finally it can be recorded that the family was made complete on 29th March 1907 by the arrival of Violet Irene Ellen Elmer, a younger sister to Florence and Wilfred. Sadly, first born Jane, only survived a few months. Both father and son died at Oxford, George in 1900 and Thomas Henry in 1947.
[See - appendix 'f' Family Tree]

A journey in excess of a century from such humble beginnings had ended with the prospect of such riches to come.

New Hinksey Girls School 1920-21

In her formative years, Violet attended the nearby New Hinksey School in Vicarage Road, the renamed Church Street. The school was known to have had a very good art teacher in Miss Louie Harding and it may be that even at this very young age Violet's spark of ability was ignited. When Miss Harding died, the pupils each took sixpence to school to buy a lamp, which was hung in the nearby church. The young Miss Elmer was born whilst the Arts and Crafts Movement and the Belle Époque in France still held sway, the Art Nouveau period was on the wane and Art Deco was still to come. There was, therefore, a plethora of styles to be absorbed in future years although it would be the art deco of the nineteen twenties and thirties that would captivate her most.

The young pupil continued her education at the Central Girls' School in New Inn Hall Street, now part of St Peter's College, University. It was during this time that the Great War was coming to an end. The Head records on 8th May 1919 "I assembled classes 1, 11, 111,1V and V1 in the hall at 11.15am this morning and read to them the important peace terms from the newspaper. I put the map up and had the new German boundaries pointed out as I proceeded". The school log recalls that vegetables collected for the Harvest Thanksgiving Festival were taken to the Town Hall, Military Hospital. There were also excursions to pick blackberries. 17lbs of fruit were used in school by the cookery teacher and the rest given to the Food Control.

Following day school and employment in her home city, Violet attended the City of Oxford College of Technology, again situated in New Inn Hall Street. However, it seems that the college used various premises in the city – a different venue for each subject. Violet first enrolled in 1922 admission number 996, address given as "Edith Road; parent at home". A second record in 1923 lists admission number 1069 dated 25th November 1923. Violet's age is recorded as 16 years. Register Reference S211/2/A7/1. Her artwork continued and the following year she completed a series of plates all bearing the reference Number FDZ/269421 presumably for a competition. The subjects included, sketches from life, wallpaper design [as seen here signed by Violet herself] and historic styles. An additional plate entitled "Design for a six frame Wilton Rug, 12 feet x 9 feet" gives a foretaste of the intricate friezes and borders that were to adorn her Best Ware ceramics in the years ahead. It would not be long before her life would change dramatically.

Sketch from life

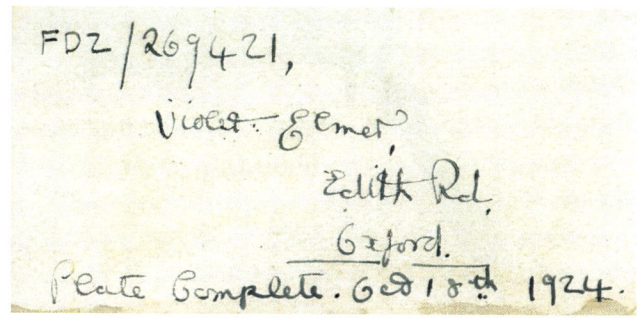

Address and signature

Historic Style

Wilton Rug

Wallpaper design

Violet and Ruby

In the same street, but a few doors away, was the birthplace of Violet's life long friend. The 1st August 1906 marked the arrival of Ruby Annie Lily, the penultimate child of Ben and Annie Moss's expansive family, Ruby's siblings being both four boys and four girls. An early friendship between Violet and Ruby was nurtured by attendance at the same New Hinksey School. Following her school days, Ruby found employment in the city, using her creative skills as a milliner at the Oxford High Street Department Store of Webbers.

During the 1920s the pair seemed inseparable, their growing relationship leading to holidays at fashionable English resorts. In 1925 it was Aberystwyth, followed in 1926 by Cowes and finally in 1927, Sheringham. The photographs confirm those happy times and illustrate fashion details of the day. That of Violet, with sketch book in hand, at Aberystwyth, is typical of those occasions.

Aberystwyth 1925

Aberystwyth 1925

Cowes, Isle of Wight 1926

Ruby - Sheringham 1927

Artistry

During this period, Violet's love of drawing and painting continued as shown in the study of her great friend "Ruby – East Cowes" signed and dated 1926. The setting and style is reminiscent of American illustrator Jessie Wilcox Smith and "Summer Day."

In 1927 the developing artist produced a series of four watercolours. The subject matter is very 'of its time' featuring fairies, pixies and ethereal creatures set in a floral landscape. The pictures bring to mind the work of illustrators such as Edmund Dulac - "The Tempest from Elves and Fairies" and Arthur Rackham - "Peter Pan in Kensington Gardens" [J.M. Barrie]. The paintings, which all retain their original labels, were professionally framed, each pair numbered 1654 and 1879 by Hills and Rowney Limited, George Street Oxford. As they were marked for each address, it is conceivable that two of them may have been a present from Violet to Ruby.

Ruby - East Cowes, dated 1926

Watercolours - 1927

Watercolours - 1927

Miss Elmer had natural artistic ability, was largely self taught and did not attend the Burslem School of Art. However, in later years, her successor, Irene Pemberton would benefit from tuition from the renowned academy. The school boasted such luminaries as Gordon Forsyth and later Reginald Haggar. Both these distinguished principals were themselves students of the Royal College of Art. Gordon Forsyth probably influenced the freehand pottery style of the late 1920s.

Ipswich born Reginald Haggar [1905-1988] originally studied at his home town School of Art. The accomplished artist, ceramic designer and lecturer, moved to Mintons in 1929 and soon established himself as Art Director, a position he held for several years. He then became Master In Charge of Stoke School of Art and subsequently the Burslem School of Art 1941-1945. Following this, he devoted his time to the painting of watercolours, writing and giving lectures. Perhaps as a contemporary of Violet Elmer, he may have made her acquaintance as these two important figures enjoyed a shared love of art deco and [in addition], both the Carlton and Minton factories were in close proximity.

The move to Carlton Ware
The late nineteen twenties brought about a change in the dynamic of the young ladies' friendship. Whilst in her late teens, Violet entered and succeeded in a major art competition. Her work, with such national and exhibition exposure, came to the attention of F.C. [Cuthbert] Wiltshaw, Managing Director of Wiltshaw and Robinson's Carlton Ware Pottery, Stoke-on-Trent. It is believed that Mr Wiltshaw wrote to Miss Elmer offering to purchase some of her paintings. However the young artist was unable to attribute a value to her work. That first contact subsequently resulted in the offer of a position of designer at the factory. Initially Violet did not wish to move from Oxford to The Potteries, her parents also being reluctant to see her leave. At the time it must have been a considerable undertaking especially for one so young. However in 1928 she made the life changing decision to leave home.

Chapter 2

The Pottery

A brief history

The much respected pottery that Violet would join was simply described in a 1922 directory as "Wiltshaw and Robinson Limited, Earthenware, China Manufacturers, Copeland Street, Stoke Central 947". Taking over relatively new premises, previously

The former pottery today

occupied by a number of ceramic enterprises, the Company was formed as a partnership in 1890. The principal founder was master potter, James Frederick Wiltshaw, born Dale Street, Burslem 22nd September 1861 and educated at Newcastle Endowed School. He began his career with his father, Thomas, at James MacIntyre and Company, Washington Works, Burslem. He had many interests at Stone where he lived with his wife Ellen, two sons and a daughter.

J. F. Wiltshaw

The other founders were the Robinson brothers from Newcastle-under-Lyme, descendants of Samuel Robinson, a school master from St Pancras, Middlesex, [b.1822 d.1864] and his wife, Sarah Alcock, a former dressmaker from Burslem, [b.1826 d.1907 or 1919]. They had moved to Lockwood Street, Newcastle following marriage. The co-founding brothers were James Alcock Robinson [b.1852 d.1931] Stoke, and William Henry Robinson [b.1854 d. 1923], Stone. James Alcock married Mary Taylor [b.1852] in 1876 with whom he had four sons. Following her death in 1908, he married Emily Brunt. Of the sons, it was the Wolstanton born, Hubert Alcock [Bute] Robinson [b.1884 d. 1966] Stoke and the redoubtable Harold Taylor Robinson [b.1877 d.1953] Derby, who enjoyed the greater lifespan. It is unclear whether Hubert, sometime of Regent Road, Trentham, was involved with the business, although he did attend J. F. Wiltshaw's funeral on the 19th August 1918.

Management difficulties were experienced regarding Harold, who joined Wiltshaw and Robinson at the turn of the century. A few years later he became a partner replacing his uncle William in the process, hence [briefly] Wiltshaw Robinson and Son. It does not appear that any members of the family of William Henry Robinson and his wife Priscilla Jane Richards were involved with the company.

In 1911, James Wiltshaw achieved a management buyout, incorporation date 13th October 1911 and consequently became the sole proprietor of the company, although the original name was retained. It seems that this was the first occasion that the concern was recorded as a limited company.

This situation continued until the 14th August 1918 when James Frederick Wiltshaw died as a result of an accident at Stoke Railway Station. He had been at the works all that day and left to catch the 6.50pm train to his home, Carlton House, Newcastle Road, Stone when the tragedy occurred.

At the funeral a few days later, with the exception of immediate mourners and Directors, over fifty employees of the firm were in attendance. Six of these acted as pallbearers. It was a considerable shock and tremendous loss for the company to lose someone of this stature, who enjoyed a great measure of personal popularity. Mr Wiltshaw was formally chairman of Stone Urban District Council and held leading positions in both Darlaston [sic] and Stone Bowling Clubs as well as the former Port Vale Athletic Club.

He was succeeded by his eldest son, Frederick Cuthbert, [b. 27.9.1892], who, relocated his family from Crewe to Stoke and assumed control of the works. Cuthbert Wiltshaw, as he became known, was a keen aviator and at the time was serving with the Forces in The Royal Flying Corps. Cuthbert proved to be a great visionary for, by the time of his retirement, he had successfully guided the pottery for almost half a century, overcoming major obstacles along the way. Perhaps his mercantile spirit and foresight should best be remembered for offering the opportunity to excel to such avant-garde designers as Enoch Boulton, Violet Elmer, Olive Kew and Irene Pemberton. The factory was driven during the 1920s and 1930s by their progressive ideas and a benchmark established for good design. At a later stage, Douglas, Cuthbert's younger brother also became a Director of the company and was an instrumental figure during the acquisition of Birks Rawlins and Company, China concern. Douglas Edward [9.6.1902-3.8.1960] was born and ultimately died at Stoke-on-Trent.

The next major difficulty which befell the manufacturer, occurred in 1931. As a result of the world wide economic crisis, the pottery found itself in Receivership. The company's bank appointed F.W. Carder as Administrative Receivers. Fortunately ensuing drastic measures had the desired effect of rendering the pottery solvent. In 1934 the Carlton Works was again endangered following the acquisition a few years earlier, of The Vine Pottery of Birks Rawlins. The drain on resources by the china enterprise resulted in another receivership issue. This time unfortunately, there was no reprieve and the Birks Rawlins enterprise was closed by the parent company. The manufactory subsequently remained under the control of the Wiltshaw family until, sadly, it lost its identity with Cuthbert's demise. The retired pottery manufacturer, of Hough Hole, Raynow, Macclesfield, died 7th July 1966 at the age of 74.

He was survived by his second wife, Edith Diggle whom he married at Macclesfield Registry Office in 1957. Considerably younger than her husband, she was the daughter of a cotton overlooker. On his death and pursuant to the powers conferred upon him by the "Articles of Association of Carlton Ware Limited", he appointed his wife as governing director. She would have the same powers, authorities and discretions as her late husband. Company director, William Goddard Purser, of Basford, Newcastle-under-Lyme, was an executor and trustee at the time .

Cuthbert's funeral was held at Carmountside Crematorium, Leek Road, Milton, Stoke-on-Trent a week later. He was described as "Governing Director of Messrs Carlton Ware, Stoke-on-Trent". With the exception of family mourners, a large number of employee's were present. His father's funeral arrangements were replicated as the six pall bearers were drawn from members of staff. There were some familiar names including one or two who had previously paid their respects to James Frederick Wiltshaw in 1918 and were now doing the same for his son.

After three-quarters of a century as an independent family concern, the company passed to Arthur Wood and Sons [Longport] Limited. Although Cuthbert and his first wife Alice [1890–1952] had several daughters and no male heir, this was not thought to be the main reason why the firm was sold. It appears that it was difficult for the remaining shareholders to decide upon the future of the company. The result was that in 1967, after Cuthbert's death, his widow [and second wife], together with the remaining Directors, had little choice but to sell the business. Although information is scarce, documents held at Companies House refer to "Carlton Ware Realisations Limited, 27th June 1967" and "Dissolved 1st November 1968".

It is recorded that in 1960, if not before, the Wood Group owned Unicorn Pottery Limited of Davenport Street, Longport. In June 1967, Unicorn changed its name to Carlton Ware Limited. The Wood Group also counted the Davenport Pottery Co. Limited; Kensington Potteries Limited and Price Brothers of Burslem, amongst their interests.

W. G. Purser

Some of the company personalities came to light at this time with the resignation of W. G. Purser in June 1969. Bill Purser was a key figure in the company. He was originally appointed as accountant in the early 1930s at the time Wiltshaw and Robinson were in recovery from receivership. Later he became finance director. It is interesting to note that following the death of his wife in 1952, Cuthbert moved away from the area. At that time, he would have been 60 years of age and following the recent turmoil in his life, may have wished to relinquish some control of the works.

Alternatively, such a development could have occurred in 1957 when the company significantly changed its name. At that time, Cuthbert would have reached the accepted retirement age of 65. It therefore seems possible that Bill Purser was promoted around 1952 and subsequently became de facto managing director and responsible for the day-to-day running of the company. Later, he became company director. As the pottery had suffered the loss of Douglas Wiltshaw in 1960, directors seemed to be in short supply. Kenneth Rollinson resigned as secretary 6th November 1970 and

Arthur Jackson took over the role the same day. It is worth noting that the Wood directors in 1977 appeared to be Gerald Francis Wood, his son Anthony Francis Wood, Arthur Wood and Son [Longport] Limited, Bradwell Works, Arthur Lloyd Jackson, sales director and Edward George Blank, works director. Arthur resigned in June 1981 as sales director and secretary and was replaced shortly after as secretary by Lee James Goddard. Edward Blank resigned as company director in September 1987.

Changes continued with Gerald Wood and Arthur Jackson resigning as directors in December 1987 upon sale of the company, still known as Carlton Ware Limited, to County Potteries PLC the same year. The purchasers' interests also included James Kent Limited, Elizabethan Fine Bone China Limited as well as Berkshire China Limited. At the same time, the company's registered office transferred to the Old Foley Pottery, King Street, Fenton.

The sale came about as a result of the struggle the company had been experiencing for some years, during depressed times; this included personal loss and allegiance to the main group. Under the grand plans of the new holding company, it was proposed to close the outdated Carlton Works and absorb the workforce into the new owner's recent acquisition of the James Kent factory. The intentions of the acquisitional County Potteries suffered a major blow when another of their recent holdings, namely the Royal Staffordshire Company had to cease trading. There followed in 1989, a brief liaison under the new name of Carlton and Kent, but to no avail. Soon after, James Kent was declared insolvent and the Carlton Ware employees were laid off. It was only through the raising of money by the managers themselves, that the last supply of coal was obtained for the heating of the premises, such was the perilous state of affairs at the famous pottery. Unfortunately a combination of poor sales, mounting debts and increasingly restrictive credit, inevitably brought about the involvement of the Receivers.

On the 15th March 1989, Price Waterhouse of Birmingham was appointed by Barclays Bank, Lombard Street, London to commence proceedings. It was not until many years later on 22nd December 1998 that the manufacturer was officially declared liquidated.

The contents of the works were disposed and the premises were sold by the Receivers to a development company. The disentangling of the web of designer attribution and many other historical facts have been hindered by the tragic loss of important documents. Upon closure, the new owners of the run down premises, not only cleared the debris but also virtually the whole of the company records. Only a few pattern books are known to have survived. This is ironic as through Cuthbert's tight control of factory proceedings, administration was safeguarded and there is no record of any fire at Copeland Street, unlike that experienced at Crown Devon.

The definitive history of the pottery, even from inception, was unfortunately lost, including details of products, staff, orders and retail outlets, indeed virtually everything. This constitutes a severe handicap to the knowledge and understanding of the company.

Thankfully, the building had been saved and put to good use. It is possible that, long term, County Potteries had seen the value in the freehold of the various sites, rather than recognising the manufacturers as ongoing productive concerns.

Although the "Carlton Ware Limited" trade name lived on, no longer would fine ceramics be produced from their original home at Copeland Street, Stoke-upon-Trent. The ultimate closure brought to an end a century of production on the same site after the founding of the company in 1890. The pottery enjoyed its greatest success during 1911-1966 whilst solely under the control of the Wiltshaw family, with a golden period being experienced from the late 1920s to the outbreak of the Second World War.

Both the Robinson and Wiltshaw families were steeped in pottery lore. For example, one of the original partners had set up W. H. Robinson, Baltimore China Works, Longton, Stoke-on-Trent. The company existed from 1901-1904 when it became known as

Robinson and Beresford. However, it was Harold Taylor Robinson who was the most renowned member of that family. He became an influential and powerful figure in the industry and held a controlling interest in many famous potteries. After leaving Wiltshaw and Robinson, Harold Taylor established J. A. Robinson and Sons Ltd., probably as a holding company for his many pottery businesses. This would later evolve into Cauldon Potteries Ltd., whose directors included his father James, together with Harold's brother Hubert, and close associate John Vivian Goddard. The company of G. L. Ashworth and Bros. Ltd., was, for many years in the ownership of the Goddard family.

At one time or another the Cauldon 'Group' comprised, amongst others Arkinstall and Sons Ltd., the maker of 'Arcadian' heraldic china. Established 1904, this was H. T. Robinson's first independent enterprise. There was also the aforementioned G. L. Ashworth and Bros., producers of Mason's Ironstone, as well as the parian manufacturer Robinson and Leadbetter. Additional acquisitions during the 1920s included Coalport, Crown Derby Porcelain, W. H. Goss, Royal Worcester and suppliers to the industry. It should be noted though, that throughout this whole period, Wiltshaw and Robinson retained their independence.

However, there were major problems ahead and the effect of the world wide recession on his companies led to the entrepreneur facing ruin and he filed for bankruptcy in 1932. As the financial liabilities of his convoluted affairs had somehow become drastically reduced, this enabled him to be released from bankruptcy in 1934. Although most of his empire had been sold off by the Receiver, his involvement with the Royal Crown Derby Porcelain Company continued, where subsequently he achieved a controlling interest. The company enjoyed considerable success as once again did its proprietor, Harold Taylor Robinson. The family relinquished control of the company in 1964.

The photograph shows, extreme left, Harold Taylor Robinson [as head of the Group] offering Cauldon china service plates to a gathering of mayors at the presentation of a banqueting service at the Kings Hall, Stoke in 1931.

Kings Hall, Stoke

The plates were designed and made by prolific modeller and designer, Sydney Richard Sanders, formerly in business at Glebe Street in Stoke-on-Trent. After the First World War however, he went to work for the Cauldon Group of companies. During the 1920s, Sydney Sanders frequently travelled with H. T. Robinson to obtain commissions from large retailers such as Burley and Company in Chicago. During these journeys they travelled well on the best ships and stayed in the grandest hotels in such cities as Chicago, Montreal, New York and Toronto. It appears that prior to Harold Taylor Robinson's financial problems of 1932, he very much enjoyed a lavish lifestyle.

The Wiltshaws were not to be outdone. Around 1892-94 Joseph Shelley Boughey and Samuel Thomas Wiltshaw were trading as Boughey and Wiltshaw in Market Street Longton. The partnership was subscquently dissolved and Samuel took over the company until 1897. Samuel Thomas [b.1864], was a brother of Carlton Ware founder, James Frederick Wiltshaw, but by 1908 had emigrated to South Africa. Incidentally, also in Market Street, as recorded in 1889, were Hibbert and Boughey.

Lifestyle
The success of the business over the years was reflected in the wherewithal of the directors. Managing director, Cuthbert Wiltshaw, was born Regent Street, Stoke-upon-Trent and was still living there at Rose Villa mid 1902. The influence he would exert on the life of Violet Elmer in the following years would be considerable. He was registered as living at Glebe House, Basford, Newcastle-under-Lyme in 1922 when he would have been thirty years of age, married, with a family. Glebe House no longer appears to exist, possibly lending its site to the present day Glebe Mews or, it may have been converted or surrendered to the whims of the traffic planners.

Up until 1928 the family appear to have been comfortably housed at "The Firs", Brampton, presently the Museum and Art Gallery, Newcastle-under-Lyme. On the 24th June 1922, William Simons of Park Place, Cardiff, sold the premises containing "two acres, four perches of land to F. C. Wiltshaw of Glebe House, Basford, Earthenware Manufacturer for £3750". This was only part of the original site, which was in excess of twelve acres. The property was relinquished by Mr Wiltshaw 2nd January 1928 in favour of Mr H. S. Adams of Lancaster Road Newcastle-under-Lyme, Provision Merchant for £4500. Designed by local architect Charles Lynam, the house was erected in 1854. It comprised, "on the ground floor, dining, drawing, breakfast rooms and kitchen, all with spacious dimensions". On the first floor, were six bedrooms and on the second floor one additional bedroom. Note that no bathroom or water closet was mentioned. Located outside, there was a coach house and stable with, as described at the time, "every suitable convenience". Pitfield House another 'grand' property stands nearby, currently used for educational purposes.

The 1891 Census declares an element of wealth in the area. As no house names are given, it is difficult to know who lived at 'The Firs' at the time. In all, six houses are enumerated at Brampton. The first was occupied by Samuel R. Edge, next was Edward Stocker China Clay Merchant then Charles Hardeman, Robert Hall Timber Merchant, followed by William S. Edwards and lastly Thomas Taylor China Manufacturer. Messrs. Edge, Hardeman and

Edwards were all listed as "living on own means".

Following a more than brief sojourn at 'The Firs', Cuthbert and family had transferred to 'The Manor House', Tittensor, Stoke-on-Trent. He was proven to be living at this address in 1930 when nearing his fourth decade and no doubt with a growing family. Whilst living there, on the 2nd June 1930 he acquired Aviators' Certificate [No.9207] from the Royal Aero Club. His profession thereon was described as "China Manufacturer". The mission was accomplished in an Avro Avian 80 h.p. Cirrus 11 aircraft at Lancashire Aero Club. Originally of all wooden construction, this

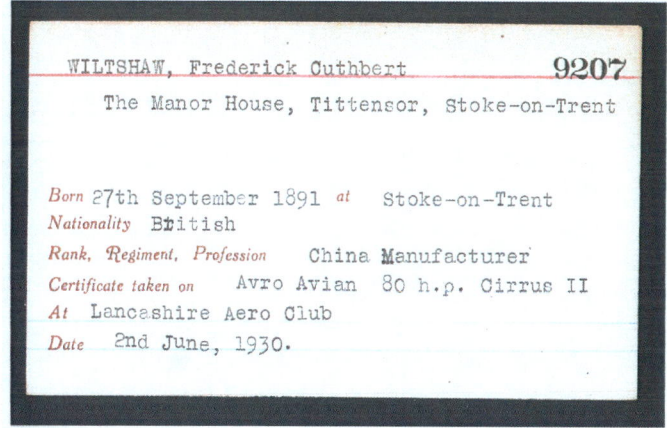

Cuthbert's Aviators Certificate and related photograph

English aeroplane was popular with many flying clubs as well as fulfilling a military flight training role. The residence, at Tittensor was the focus of his family for a relatively short period, the premises have since been demolished.

If the telephone directory is to be believed, Court Dreve, Weeping Cross, Milford, Staffordshire played host in 1933. The briefness of the stay is only equalled by the knowledge available.

The twelve room villa of 'Estoril', Station Road, Barlaston was named by Cuthbert and his wife Alice after a favourite Iberian resort which they visited on many occasions. From probably as early as 1934 to certainly 1952, this was the home they shared together until, Cuthbert's wife and mother of his daughters tragically died before her time. Alice would have been sixty two years of age. It was July in 1952 that her body was discovered by her husband in the hallway of their family home. The savagery of the attack stunned not only the local neighbourhood but people nationally. The manhunt was led by Detective Superintendent Reginald Spooner of Scotland Yard. Jewellery to the value of £3500 was stolen during the daytime raid. Many statements were taken including some from relatives and staff at 'Estoril'. However, the one exception was Leslie Green, 29 years of age who was formerly employed by the Wiltshaws. Soon after, he walked into a Police Station to account for his movements and deny the murder. Green, who was known to the police, had in the past worked as a chauffeur and gardener and had stolen from previous employers. Apparently, the chauffeur had been dismissed by the Wiltshaw's for using the car when the family were on holiday.

He was held for theft, charged and found guilty of murder at his trial at Stafford. Despite protestations of innocence to the end, he was hanged at Winson Green Prison, Birmingham on December 23rd 1952. Understandably after this dreadful event, Cuthbert Wiltshaw sold the property and moved away to Macclesfield. Today 'Estoril' is an annexe to the Wedgwood Memorial College and Conference Centre, Stoke-on-Trent.

There is limited knowledge concerning Cuthbert's younger brother and director, Douglas [D. E.] Wiltshaw regarding his life sans Copeland Street. However, in 1933 he was known to be residing with his wife Florence Foster at 'Byways', Dairy Fields, Trentham, Stoke-on-Trent. In 1939, at the age of thirty seven, he was living nearby at 'The Parkway', Dairy Fields. The area has changed with consequent residential development. Finally, a reference to an address at Cross Heath, Newcastle-under-Lyme has been found. Douglas was well liked at the works and regarded as a "man of the people", whereas his elder brother was believed to be more reserved. Cuthbert was certainly saddled with a heavy burden of responsibility.

Cuthbert Wiltshaw c.1952

Of the other directors, the brothers James Alcock and William Henry Robinson are first recorded living with their parents at Shaw Street, Newcastle-under-Lyme in 1861. A few years later the situation had dramatically changed following the death of their father. Their mother Sarah, still in her thirties, had been left with a family of six young children. The sadness was compounded in that the first born, Frances Ann, had died in 1859 at the age of eight years. As with the Elmers, families in those days suffered their share of infant mortality. How difficult it must have been for both the courageous Sarah and the children. In 1871 they were all still at home at Shelton New Road Newcastle, under the care of their widowed mother. Thankfully those of suitable age were gainfully employed. James was described as 'writing clerk', whilst his brother William had become an apprentice to an ironmonger. By 1881, Sarah Robinson had moved the family, including William, to Liverpool Road, Newcastle. Later changes of address to firstly

Albert Terrace, Wolstanton, [Newcastle-under-Lyme] and secondly, Rock Lodge, Hartshill Road, Stoke, ensued.

Following marriage in 1876, James Alcock moved to Newport Street, Burslem and then to Emberton Street, Wolstanton. Both Park Cottage and Silverdale Road, claimed him in 1891 and 1901 respectively. Incidentally, son Hubert in 1901, was described as a 'potters' writing clerk' – it must have run in the family. Circumstances had changed for James as in 1911, he was living with his new wife Emily, in some style, at the Gothic fifteen roomed Dunwood Hall, Endon, Stoke-on-Trent. Although by now his children had all left home, James' brother, Arthur Arkinstall [Robinson] was living with them. Both James, now aged 58 and Arthur aged 49, single, described themselves as 'china, earthenware manufacturers'. It appears that Arthur had several career moves ranging from the popular ironmongery trade, commercial traveller, to earthenware manufacture. Three servants lived in at Dunwood Hall, a cook, domestic and groom/coachman. As early as 1912, James was linked with premises known as The Quarry, Hartshill, Stoke, the address where his death was recorded in 1931.

Soon after marriage in 1887, William and his wife were found registered as 'visitors' at Victoria Road, North Portsea, Portsmouth. As his host was described as a commercial traveller in the provisions trade, perhaps this was a business connection. According to a listing in a directory of 1900, William Henry next appears at Silverdale Road, a familiar address at Wolstanton. What is not in dispute however, is that in 1901, William now 46, described as China Manufacturer [earthenware], was living with his wife and four children, at 'Harewood', Forsbrook, near Stoke. The family had become prosperous, as in their employ was a governess, servant and a groom cum gardener. A decade later the family still occupied the same premises, probably William's final home. Some of the details bear amplification as by 1911, William had changed his occupation to commercial traveller [china] and son Douglas, at 18, was employed by The Potteries Electric Tramways as an engineer.

Harold Taylor Robinson, the scion of the family, was born at Newport Street, Burslem and lived with his parents at Park

Cottage, Silverdale Road, Wolstanton. In 1910, he married Kathleen Olive Farrington and moved to Brook Street, Stoke-on-Trent. It is curious that there also appears to be a listing at about the same time at Queens Road, Penkhull, Stoke. He was already describing himself at the age of 33 as a 'china manufacturer'. Things were obviously going well, for, at his house in Brook Street, he and his wife were already employing two members of staff. At this time there was no doubt, an element of management turmoil at the Copeland Street Works. He was next connected in 1930 with a property at Mucklestone, near Market Drayton. Much later in his life, he moved to The Uplands, Manor Road, Derby, where he died at the age of 75.

It is intriguing to see how some of the founding families rose from quite modest beginnings to enjoy considerable prosperity. It should be taken into account that families moved house far more frequently than they do today. Houses were usually rented; people often moved when there was a birth or death in the family, when they got married or set up on their own. A move further up the street was not uncommon. There were no contracts or tenants rights and the poor, perhaps behind with the rent, moved at the 'drop of a hat' or if necessary, did a 'moonlight flit'. The wealthy moved less often as they usually owned their houses.

[See appendix 'g' 'Descendants of James Robinson']

What is in a Name
Although the word 'Carlton' is inextricably interwoven into the fabric of the pottery, its origin in company terms may be unknown. It does however, conjure up an appropriate image of prestige, quality and of the very best. Its usage virtually throughout the history of the business related to the name of the firm itself, its trademark, the back-stamp logo as well as the identity of the works. It should also be remembered that co-founder James Frederick Wiltshaw lived at Carlton House, Stone and although evidence is not conclusive, it would appear that the house was named after the factory rather than vice versa.

Shortly after establishment, Wiltshaw and Robinson adopted the slogan 'Carlton Ware' and this usage continued for some sixty years. It is generally recognised that in 1957, the company changed its name to reflect this, as officially confirmed 8th January 1958. Thought to have been registered in 1893, the earliest documentary evidence of the firm's famous "Carlton Ware" Trade Mark, was in 1894, when the emblem was incorporated into the Crown Swallow backstamp. As early as 1902 products were being advertised under the "Carlton Ware" banner with further confirmation of this in 1911.

The premises
The year 1863 marked the laying of the first bricks of what would ultimately become, in 1890, the factory and headquarters of the world renowned ceramic enterprise.

The premises, initially known as The Copeland Street Works were built for Turner and Wood, names connected with some of the famous Staffordshire potters. The building was occupied by a succession of companies. Previous incumbents were thought to be manufacturers of ceramic items for the burgeoning electricity industry, together with door knobs and finger plates. Such evidence as exists points to the name being changed to "Carlton Works" shortly before the turn of the century. By reference to the ordnance survey of 1877, the factory is found described as '"Parian Manufactory" and fronting the significantly named Copeland Street

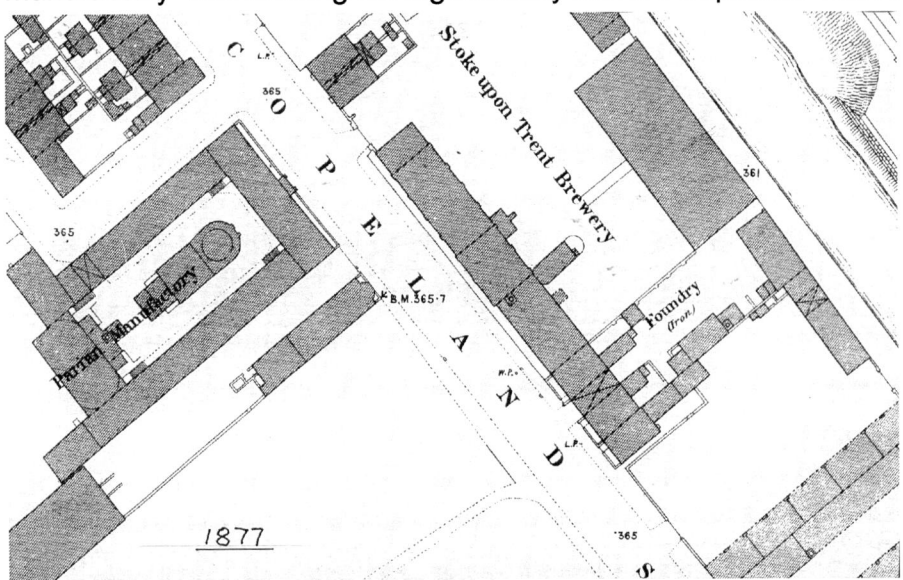

Parian Manufactory

in much the same way as today. The 1924 survey describes the premises "Carlton Works, Earthenware". Only a small pedestrian

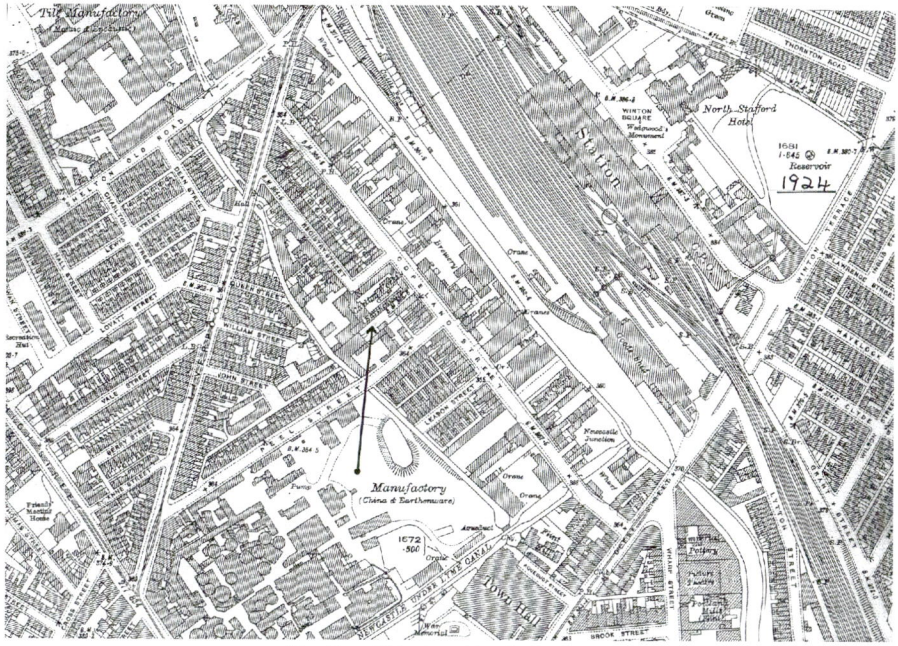
Carlton Works, Earthenware

entrance abuts Copeland Street itself. The factory's long return frontage to Baring Street, now part of Registry Street, contained the main vehicular, goods and artisans' tunnel entrance. The lodge

The Works Entrance

keeper would carefully monitor all movements in and out of the building. This employee had important additional duties appertaining to time keeping and arrangements for the taking on of extra workers or casual labour.

The immediate area was highly developed at this time, with, on the opposite side of Copeland Street, Stoke-upon-Trent Brewery and an adjoining iron foundry, now all but a distant memory beneath subsequent highway development. To the south-east the land was undeveloped but to the north-west the intensive development of the Registry Street area painted a different picture. The site benefited from good transport links, with the mid 19th century Stoke Railway Station, the scene of James Frederick's tragic accident, a stone's throw away.

It may be that Miss Elmer alighted from the train here on her journey to work, having boarded at the long lost Newcastle Station in Kings Street. Also conveniently located, is the late eighteenth century Trent and Mersey Canal, with, nearby, the now defunct offshoot to Newcastle-under-Lyme. To the rear of the site is Fowlea Brook, a tributary of the River Trent which it joins nearby. The Trent from its source near Biddulph, here begins its perambulations towards the Humber.

The Iconic Chimney

As to the building itself, the three-story structure surrounds a traditional central courtyard containing the prominent chimney with additional buildings at the back. The 'island site' contains the boiler house and the original depository of the factory records.

Regarding the main block, the layout was labyrinthine over the three floors. The placement of stairways was confusing with quite a number leading directly off individual rooms. Designers, paintresses, enamellers, gilders et al. would have needed the best natural light. They were accommodated on both the first and second floors and applied their skills to good purpose by utilising the numerous large windows, particularly on the north western side.

Interior View - present day

The office and boardroom of the managing director, was on the first floor, adjacent to the northern corner and that of director Douglas Wiltshaw, situated through the tunnel, on the ground floor to the left. With the exception of the clay end, most of the related craftspeople, tradesmen and office staff would have been housed in the rest of the premises. For example, following entry through the lodge, the aerography department would have been found to the right with two others upstairs, one of which was on the top floor. The glaze department was also on the top floor. Colour departments, where the paint was mixed were located on both ground and first floors. Prior to the Second World War, Stanley Nixon was general manager and responsible for the production of colours for the decorating shop. It is also believed that in addition to this important role, he possessed the closely guarded secret formula of rouge royale. The biscuit warehouse was on the ground floor. At the far end of the aerography shop on the first floor, was to be found the show room or shop. The packing warehouse was also on this floor. It has been said that one of the most fascinating areas were the large dark mould chambers on the second floor. The glost warehouse was thought to be situated on the top floor and the large basement was also utilised in the manufacturing process. Within the buildings adjacent to the brook, raw materials would have been processed into the usable clay element prerequisite of the modeller, moulder and caster. With the exception of the original bottle ovens, the warehouse and some buildings to the rear, the fulcrum of creativity survives largely intact. However, the interior today reveals little of the illustrious past, other than possibly a bricked up kiln arch and a fragment of rail-track in the area of the old casting shop at the clay end. Alas, there is no sign of the original engine house.

The current usage of the building is light industrial on the ground floor with a further refurbishment of the remainder for use by university students. The rearmost part is fulfilling the purpose of furniture store and most appropriately an antique business.

Kilns
Bottle ovens were the mainstay of the potteries for centuries and even as late as 1960 many hundreds remained, although the use of coal had ceased. Previous to Wiltshaw and Robinson days, the ordnance survey of 1877 purports to show two such kilns at the Copeland Street Victorian pot bank which possibly formed an integral part of a building. However, superior evidence exists in the form of an aerial survey film taken by the RAF 11th August 1945. This distinctly shows two bottle ovens to the rear of the courtyard. It is thought that they could have been used in tandem for a while with the new electric kilns. Upon entry through the factory tunnel, one bottle oven was to the right approached through the aerography shop and the other by the clay department.

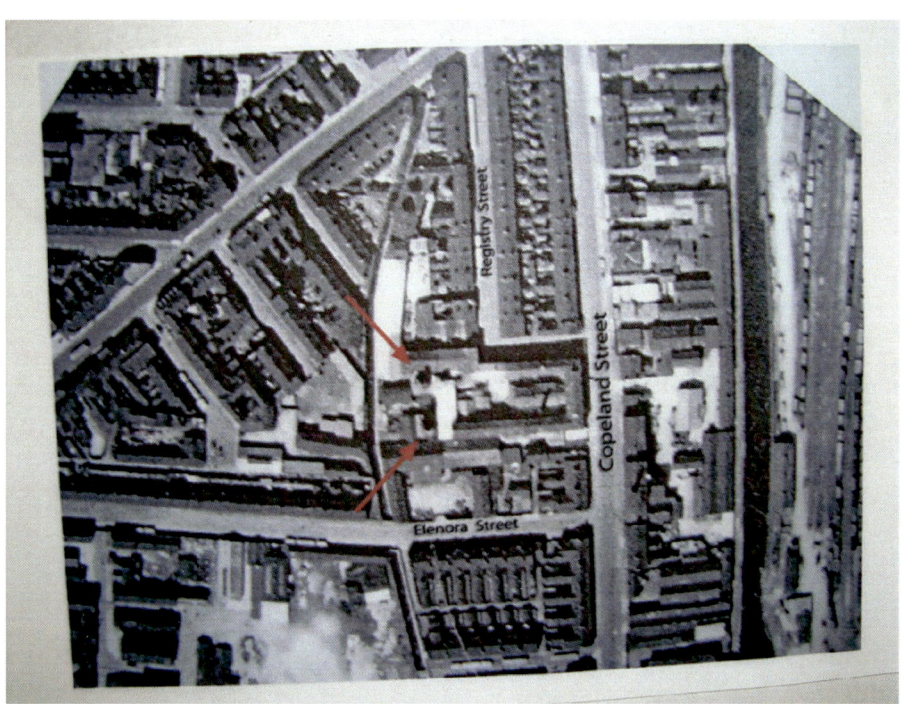
Bottle Ovens 1945

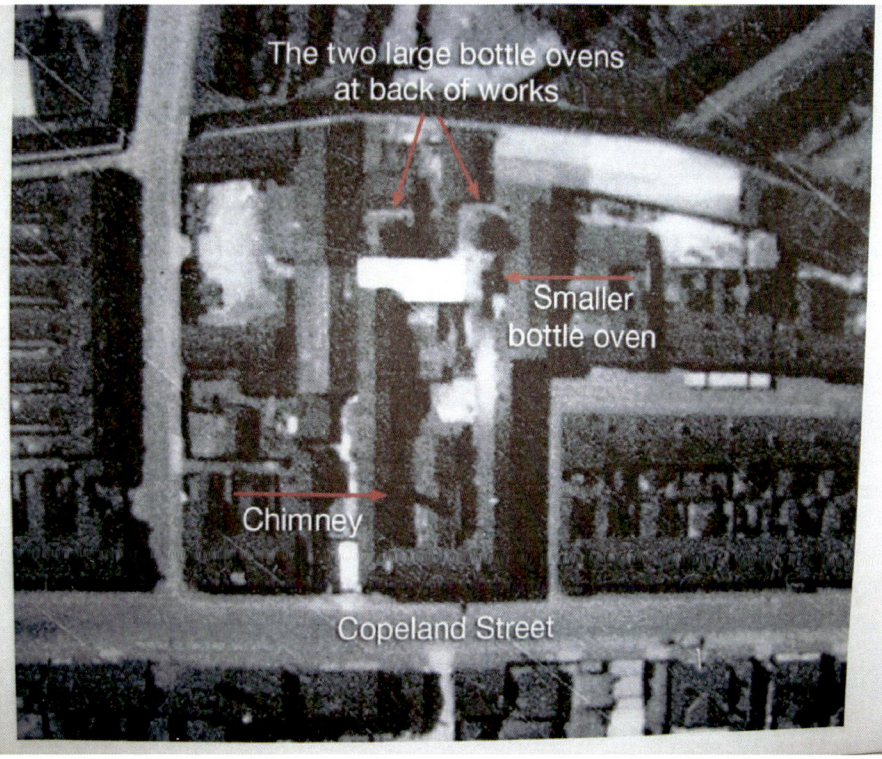
Bottle Ovens 1945

The industry owes a considerable debt to Conrad Dressler [1856-1940] for showing the way forward. He revolutionised how firing took place during the early part of the twentieth century. An English sculptor, aesthete and art potter of Teutonic ancestry, he was founder of the Medmenham Pottery which produced, inter alia, handcrafted architectural tiles and panels of distinction. Conrad Dressler was a disciple of William Morris and the Arts and Crafts movement as well as being an admirer of William de Morgan.

However, around the turn of the century the decline of sales resulted in the discontinuation of his business. In order to support his family, art was reluctantly sacrificed to pure inventiveness.

Dressler's discovery of a white glazed tile, suitable for use within industry and hospitals, demanded a method of mass production not available at the time. His concept of a tunnel oven, comprising a central combustion chamber with moving cars on tracks containing the ware and propelled slowly through the chamber, came about as early as 1908. This continuous heating method radically changed the industry. Subsequent improvements were made and after its initial use in the refractory trade, his invention slowly gained favour in the pottery industry as a whole. The new system was only fully adopted after the hostilities of the Second World War, because there were also constraints of traditionalism, cost and space.

Post war, in common with most of the English ceramic manufacturers, Carlton Ware modernised with the introduction, in 1946, of a new electric glost kiln and two years later, a 'Dressler type' electric tunnel biscuit oven. Anecdotal evidence suggests that many years later, there were several kilns located on different floors with attendant groups of craftspeople and paintresses working on separate lines of production.

Workforce, Sales and New Designs
The Carlton Works was a relatively small pottery when compared to the likes of Wedgwood, Doulton and Spode, which supplied the mass market. What it lacked in capacity, it made up for in resourcefulness and adaptability. The plant's skilful workforce was

known to be happy, loyal and conscientious, it being not unusual for different generations of the same family to serve the company a lifetime. Violet Elmer would have enjoyed these pleasurable working conditions. In relation to the very busy chapter during the late nineteen thirties, the personnel had risen to well in excess of three hundred souls, a number that was almost matched in 1960.

In 1938 the twenty first birthday of Betty, eldest daughter of Cuthbert and Alice Wiltshaw, was celebrated at Hanley with a party for all the members of staff. Miss Wiltshaw held a responsible position in the design department at the works. It was the first time in the history of the pottery that the entire sales staff had been assembled in one place. The guests included Mr Barlow, the firm's Australian representative, who had served the company in one of its principal markets for twenty two years. F. R. Barlow and Sons were to be found in Melbourne at 328 Flinders Street, a substantial building, which is now an hotel. Mr Harry Davis, the firm's northern agent took responsibility for organising the evening. Mrs. Coomer, the firm's oldest employee, presented the late Betty Cornes [née Wiltshaw] with a gift on behalf of the staff. [See photograph on page 168.]

To extol the virtue of the workforce and recognise the personalities who made such a contribution to the pottery during the nineteen twenties and thirties is of paramount importance. Records are included of those employees known, many of whom would have been colleagues and friends of Miss Elmer. Additional records of some of those who joined after the outbreak of the Second World War, are also shown.
[see appendices 'c', 'd' and 'e']

There were strict regulations for the workers. Prior to the last World War, rules were in place which forbade workers to contact those in a department other than their own. This seems draconian today.

Wiltshaw and Robinson did not lack ambition, with the promotion of products a high priority. As well as a regional sales force, showrooms were to be found at the pottery itself as well as in London. The former colonies were well served with main agents in Australia, Canada, New Zealand and South Africa. In Europe, the company was represented in Belgium, Denmark, France, Holland, Italy, Portugal and Switzerland. Other outlets existed in America, Argentina, Brazil, Venezuela and even Hong Kong. Some representatives regularly visited the Stoke-on-Trent factory. It is regrettable that only comparatively recently, has the work of individual designers become more widely recognised. The export market to Australia, in all things Carlton Ware, was particularly buoyant and accounted for a large proportion of sales. Indeed some of the most magnificent Best Ware collections are still to be found in that country today.

New lines would be shown at relevant trade fairs and exhibitions, as well as advertised in fashionable magazines and trade journals such as The Pottery Gazette and Glass Trade Review. To elucidate, the company was listed as exhibitor at the British Industries Fair, held at the White City, London 18th February to 1st March 1929. Described as a "Manufacturer of Decorative Pottery", it was allocated stand number G44. Not unlike today, the business was also quick to seize the opportunity to exploit national celebrations such as a royal wedding or anniversary. For instance, in 1937 the company produced a limited edition jug and boxed medallion to celebrate the 70th anniversary of the Confederation of Canada.

Confederation Jug

The product range, in terms of availability and quality was outstanding. Prior to the Second World War, it appears that the Best Ware range was virtually made to order, thereby saving on unnecessary costs and wastes. Only small batches were made, perhaps even as few as a dozen at a time. Vases or other artefacts bearing the rarest patterns were costly to produce, expensive to buy and consequently had a limited market. New patterns or shapes, by, say, Violet Elmer, would be submitted to management and possibly a sample made. A decision as to production would then be taken by Mr Cuthbert Wiltshaw, in conjunction with the opinion of the salesmen. The sales staff were important as they were well versed with the market place and competitors' products and therefore adept at providing Carlton's management with valuable information. If the decision was affirmative, the new product line would be added to the salesman's brochure. He would then approach various retailers in an endeavour to obtain orders.

Not all designs were accepted and those rejected would not receive a pattern number and would be disposed of. Several examples are known to exist and being unique, can become quite valuable as well as being historically interesting. It is known that a master potter's family could be given the 'trials' once they had been either put into production or shelved as a 'not for market' product. Carlton's commercial salesmen, travelling as they did in the nineteen thirties by rail, would approach suitable mid size retailers and only then, when orders had been obtained, would production proceed. Other potteries adopted similar methods, producing an initial batch of about a dozen ceramic samples for the salesmen to use. Only a proportion of the many designs submitted were manufactured. Small production runs, loss and damages over the years, would account for the scarcity of so many iconic patterns. Today's collectors are presented with an admirable degree of difficulty, for as well as cost and condition, the source is finite. Custodians are therefore charged with considerable responsibility and it may take them a lifetime to find an elusive piece.

Wiltshaw and Robinson were primarily renowned as makers of floral and fruit embossed products which still exist in large numbers. The second generation goods of abstract, geometric, art deco and fantasy design have also withstood the test of time remarkably well and are still in vogue today. In its day, for most people, a top Best Ware piece would account for a major portion of their weekly wage.

The Best Ware products could be identified by the factory's small circular paper label. Two sets of numbers were shown: the uppermost being the four-digit pattern number, whilst that below related to shape and size of product. For instance, a label bearing 3447 above 456/6, would enable a retailer to re-order a six inch vase in the matt **Explosion** pattern on shape 456.

The presentation of Best Ware remains unexplained, as no evidence of boxes or packaging has been found. In general, the means of moving ware from the pottery to retail outlets, was by large cartons or wooden barrels filled with straw [hogshead]. This method existed at least until the 1950s.

Although the decorative products of some well-known potteries are all too easily recognised, this cannot be said of Wiltshaw and Robinson's top of the range output. The originality, colour range and exceptional detail, elevates the Best Ware brand to a level in keeping with the very best English producers. The demise of the skill base, labour intensive processes, combined with the fickleness of fashion and modern economics, leads to the conclusion that such high quality products, as Carlton's exuberant Best Ware will never again be produced.

Public Utilities
The earliest gas supplier was a private company at Shelton, possibly supplying Hanley and Stoke with street lighting in 1825. Progress was made and in the 1840s a supply was available to several factories, Inns and houses. The original private undertakings were of a somewhat piecemeal nature and were taken over by the Public Authority around 1880 and consolidated into public ownership after the turn of the century.

It was a similar story regarding the supply of electricity, with the first evidence of its availability being c.1894, under the auspices

ANOTHER LOAD OF *Carlton Ware*

You will appreciate the cartons we use for packing. They are so much cleaner and easier to handle.

AGENTS

Australia : F. R. Barlow & Sons (Pty.) Ltd., Commerce House, 328 Flinders Street, Melbourne, C.I.
New Zealand : Aubrey Gualter & Co., P.O. Box No. 625, Wellington, C.I.
London : S. Prior, 9 Charterhouse Street, E.C.I.
Canada : Oakley, Jackson & Farewell, Ltd., No. 2, Leader Lane (at 32, Wellington Street, E.), Toronto, 2.
South Africa : A. C. McIntosh Pty., Ltd., P.O. Box No. 3081, Johannesburg.

WILTSHAW & ROBINSON LTD., Carlton Works, Stoke-on-Trent

Pottery Gazette - 1940

of the Hanley Electricity Works. Regarding Stoke and Burslem, the Borough Council initiated matters in 1904 with the opening of the electricity works in Bagnall Street [now Yeoman Street]. This facility was extended in 1911. Incidentally, Stoke-upon-Trent Station and part of the North Stafford Hotel were first lit by electricity as early as 1893. Following confederation, a uniform system of supply and consolidation of the previous individual Provisional Orders was achieved by the Stoke-on-Trent Corporation Act of 1923. As electricity was introduced to the nearby Spode Factory the same year, it follows that a similar time frame existed regarding Carlton Ware, number 46 Copeland Street. This no doubt took over from the existing gas arrangement. Matters continued at a pace in the electricity industry with state control bringing about commencement of the national grid in 1928 with completion in 1933.

There were many trials and tribulations at Stoke during the 19th century concerning public health, drainage and water supply until satisfactory arrangements were eventually made.

Note: Throughout this book, the pattern names given in upper case are those named by the factory. Those in lower case, originate from the Naming Committee of the former Carlton Ware Collectors Clubs. The same design would often have been produced in a different colourway. As each colourway and any variation to the main pattern would have been allocated its own individual pattern number, the book does not claim to be totally comprehensive in this respect.

Chapter 3

Products 1890 – 1938

A Broad Overview

The multifarious products, which originated from the factory formed numerous categories. There were the purely decorative items, which the company produced in various forms throughout its history, together with a staple diet of very successful tableware. Novelty items and advertising ware were also manufactured over a long period. Whether it was the decorative or everyday functional, the pottery was very adept at embracing change and sought to achieve the highest product quality. Most of the early items leant heavily on the style of the more established potteries. Carlton Ware, as it later officially became known, produced its own interpretations of blush ware and the related, more sophisticated variants, such as blue and white, flow blue and imari. At this time, there was also sprigged ware, a derivation of that produced by Wedgwood. Heraldic china made its début just after the turn of the century and was another successful Carlton brand produced over several decades.

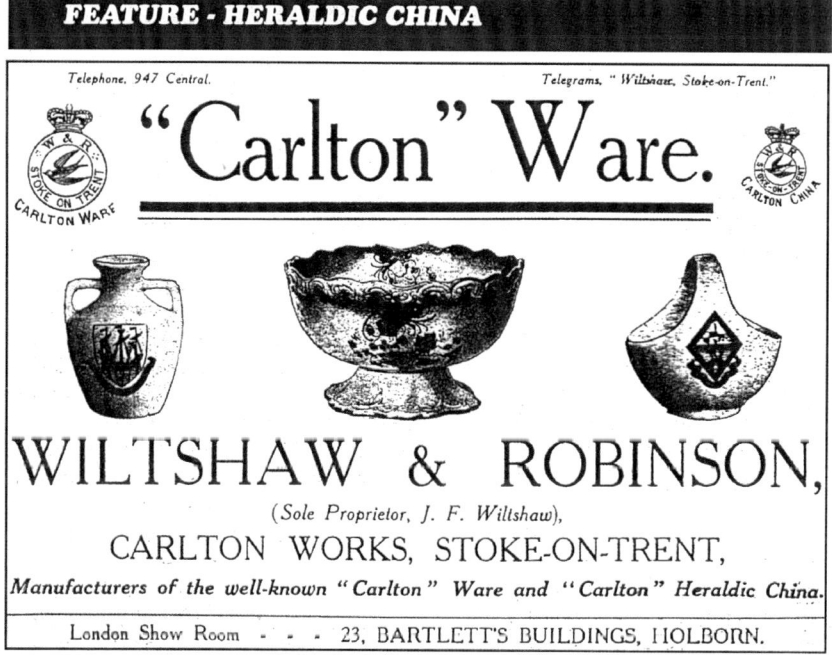

1911 Advertisement

Pieces reflecting the late Victorian and Edwardian era were, in some cases, surprisingly elegant. Well moulded shapes, an abundance of floral designs, gilding and considerable attention to detail were evident. Indeed some pieces, such as vases, bowls, or plates finished in a combination of blues, red and white, were positively lavish. During this period, cloisonné ware was available usually to be found on a matt black ground and quite often featuring birds and prunus designs. The very Victorian **PEACH BLOSSOM** [2030] was another design well to the fore. Ranges such as the long standing chinoiserie with all its variations and **TUTANKHAMEN** [2711] had already come to the marketplace.

PEACH BLOSSOM

TUTANKHAMEN

The development within this decade would continue at a pace, with 1925 marking the arrival of salad ware. This line together with the later famous fruit and floral embossed ranges co-existed for many years, alongside the ornamental products. No doubt the everyday commercial tableware items, subsidized the more elaborate products which were expensive to manufacture.

It would now be only a few years before Miss Elmer would enter a hotbed of activity. Examples of salad ware, comprised such items as bowls, modelled in the form of a lettuce leaf with red tomato feet, or alternatively resting on lobster claws. The design and quality of

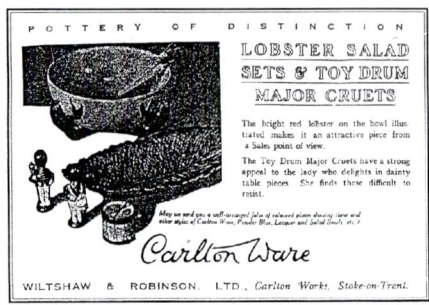
1927 Advertisement

these products, as with the later fruit and floral embossed ware, rendered them almost beyond use. There were exciting times towards the close of the 1920s with the birth of Carlton's China Tea Ware and the Handcraft range which led to the formation of the company's renowned Best Ware of the 1930s.

The variation of output was immense. For example, an attractive pearlised lustre Orange Ware breakfast set, which was suitably embossed with oranges and leaves, colourful fruit preserves in relief, souvenir items, comical napkin rings, cruets and other

Queen Mary and the Queen of Sweden have purchased Carlton Lacquer Ware.

22/6 Morning Set, No Tray
34/3   „   „   With Tray

CARLTON ORANGE WARE

This illustration of a morning set shows how delightful your pottery can be. You should go to your Pottery Shop and ask to see this new Carlton Orange Ware. The motif of the decoration is realistically embossed, oranges and green leaves — a fresh combination of colours that lends a most cheerful and inspiring atmosphere to the table.

Carlton Ware is, of course, as rich in quality as it is in colouring. The many pieces that are available in this Orange design are moderately priced and will give you years of service. Compare by prices—by quality—or by general appearance, and your choice will ultimately be Carlton.

May we send you coloured illustrations? Write for name of nearest supplier, also folio of coloured plates showing decorative pieces, Salad Bowls and Coffee Sets, etc., to Dept. G.

WILTSHAW & ROBINSON LTD
CARLTON WORKS.   STOKE - ON - TRENT

1927 Advertisement

fancies. No better example can be given of the pottery's ingenuity than the contrast between these items and the revolutionary 'oven to table ware' in 1929. Techniques such as drip glaze and tubelining were explored. In the late 1930s, the company flirted with the French influenced 'Glacielle', ornamental ware which mainly featured studies of animals, in a unique simulated finish reminiscent of stippled ice. Not for the first time a product achieved royal patronage. In addition, figurines, comical novelty dogs and similar in a ribbed stoneware format left the factory.

Another of the many diverse products which emanated from the Copeland Street premises, were musical tankards, a sign that the company was well in tune with current trends. The list lengthened with 'Cottage Ware' being added in the mid 1930s together with its partner, 'Rock Garden'. Thematic, functional, tableware was also plentiful. This period in the long history of Wiltshaw and Robinson's undertaking would bow out, with amongst others, sets of posy holders. Their design was inspired by flowers such as the crocus, lily and poppy, which were modelled in relief with naturalistic colours.

It is necessary on occasion to exercise caution regarding production dates. A newly conceived design might not have been produced immediately and indeed, in some cases, could have been delayed for some years. It must not be forgotten that production runs could vary enormously depending on the popularity or otherwise of the product.

Chapter 4

Horace Wain Designer 1911 – c.1921

Chinoiserie and Armand

With Violet Elmer now in her infancy, little knowing of her illustrious future, it was perhaps surprising that the firm she was later to join had yet to employ a full time 'in house' designer. However, in 1911 this was rectified when, following the takeover of the pottery by James Frederick Wiltshaw, this vital position was filled by the appointment of Horace Wain [1886-1967]. One of his earliest accreditations is **REPRODUCTION SWANSEA CHINA** [624] the Wiltshaw's acknowledgement to the Swansea factory's 19th century design. Not long after this, the designer who gave the company a new direction, commenced work on what would become one of the most popular and long-lived marques ever produced at the factory. Carlton Ware, not the only company at the time to have a fixation with the Orient, introduced the Chinoiserie range, the original Best Ware, featuring especially the Mikado pattern. The coming of this new style, reflecting as it did, imitations of Chinese motifs, would unfortunately be interrupted by the impending First World War.

Advertisement for chinoiserie

Products during the period of hostilities like those after the death of Queen Victoria, tended to be of a sober, less colourful nature in keeping with the times. For instance, ceramics reflecting this, featured birds and flowers within a cartouche, displayed on a sombre black matt ground. Towards the end of the war, Armand was brought to the attention of the buying public, a product with its own distinctive back stamp. Vases and ginger jars in this unique high glaze format, usually in light blue or a polychromatic surface texture, displayed cockerels flowers and insects. At about the same time, the rich enamelling of **ROCKERY AND PHEASANT** [2071] and **COCK and PEONY** [2250] were presented by the company.

COCK AND PEONY Armand

After the laying down of arms, the development of Chinoiserie continued with **MIKADO** [1883] and **TEMPLE** [2367] to the fore. Predominant ground colours were red or blue although other options were available. There was a corresponding choice of finish. An infinite number of shapes were used within this ubiquitous category which were still available well after the Second World War. These came in all forms and sizes including appropriately, temple jars. Towards the end of Horace Wain's term, patterns were becoming less traditional and formal, giving a foretaste of what was to come. In 1921, having made a valued contribution to the pottery, he would leave to join A. G. Harley-Jones and Company, the manufacturers of Wilton Ware. Many years later, he had a strong association with H. Wain and Sons Limited of Longton who produced embossed earthenware and novelties under the 'Melba Ware' trademark.

Pattern Numbers 3274 & 3527 shape 125

The luxury side of the business was at a crossroads in the late 1920s following the effect of the Paris Exhibition. This necessitated a major redesign examination of the goods currently made at the works. A new product was required to link the more traditional patterns with the new age format, in order to compete with the more innovative potteries. Britain generally, including no doubt Wiltshaw and Robinson, adopted a somewhat restrained reaction to the new style and took time to assess the situation.

S. Fielding and Company

At the end of 1929 and after the best part of a decade of excellent service, Enoch Boulton, along with commercial manager, George Eli James Barker, of Oak Hill, Stoke-on-Trent, resigned. They were soon to join S. Fielding and Company, makers of the Crown Devon brand where Enoch was appointed chief designer and decorating manager and George, sales director. Although it is difficult to say, it doesn't appear that Fieldings deliberately courted the couple or enticed them away. The pair seemed to have become disenchanted with the personal impact of the financial problems being experienced at Copeland Street at the time.

Chapter 7

The Art Deco Years

The Paris Exhibition
The movement that would impact on the pottery, and in time, have a profound effect on Violet Elmer, would become known, some time later, as Art Deco. This was ostensibly a European happening with its roots found pre-war in Art Nouveau and Modernism. Art Deco would reflect the wondrous sets and costumes of Diaghilev's Ballets Russes. The avant-garde theatre company caught the imagination of Paris from 1909 with its unconventional approach and works based on ethnic, oriental and radical themes. The new Russian development would endure and influence other forms of art. A few years later, the German Bauhaus Movement would provide additional direction.

There was a desire after the First World War, for change and a wish, in France, to re-establish pre-eminent French taste, in an increasingly industrialised new world. Paris in 1925 was most significant as the showcase of the new movement. The Exposition Internationale des Arts Décoratifs et Industriels Modernes attracted exhibitors from many countries and lit the touchpaper for even greater events to follow.

The new movement was empowered, amongst others, by artistic characteristics of Africa, Egypt, and Greece; strong elements were also borrowed from early native America. Carlton Ware's Enoch Boulton and Violet Elmer would utilize the geometric formulae which had its routes in Aztec, Inca and Mayan culture. Sunbursts, zig zags and lightning flashes would all be represented in their work. The sensational new style with appropriate colourings was expressed as a distinctive, clean, sleek, glitzy and simplified form indicative of the spirit and glamour of the times. It would influence all art forms world wide. Ceramics, fashion, furniture, glass, interior design, jewellery, metalwork, graphics, sculpture and textiles all embraced the modern design. Luxury travel was also included and many examples would be found in motor cars, grand hotels, and ocean liners.

Cinema

It was not surprising though, that there was a certain reluctance to completely abandon the past and a blend of styles would continue for some time. The Gaumont Theatre in Ipswich, Suffolk, one of the many new cinemas being built at the time, which opened in 1929, is one such example. This opulent palace, boasting a commissionaire, electric lighting, Wurlitzer organ, eighteen piece orchestra and a manager's cottage to the rear, made the premises unique. Capable of catering for nearly two thousand people, a front circle seat at the first performance cost two shillings and four pence. If desired, tea could be served from the luxurious restaurant to any of the fourteen boxes, located to the rear of the stalls. Whilst the auditorium is rather utilitarian, it is however, embellished with lighting of the period. The crush area is quite different, for as can be seen, although broadly accepting the new style, remnants of the more traditional remain.

Interior Gaumont Theatre Ipswich

Interior Gaumont Theatre Ipswich

North America

Architectural examples abound in Europe, Shanghai, some South American cities and Napier, the Art Deco City of New Zealand. Even Japan had its own interpretation of the genre. The new style took on a whole new meaning when it crossed the Atlantic, where the revolution was exploited in all forms of life and architecture. It epitomised the age of conspicuous consumption and flourished in North America long after it waned in Europe in the late 1930s. Above all, some of the best architectural examples were to be seen in California, Miami in Florida and the imposing skyscrapers of Manhattan in New York.

Chapter 8

Carlton China Tea Ware

Birks Rawlins and Company

Although mainly known as a manufacturer of earthenware, in 1928, Wiltshaw and Robinson enlarged their product base by the takeover of the struggling Vine Pottery run by Birks Rawlins & Co. This pottery, manufactured porcelain and bone china products, including tea settings. The acquisition was largely orchestrated by Cuthbert's younger brother and co-director, Douglas E. Wiltshaw. The Company had existed for almost four decades, having been founded in 1894. The pottery was located less than a mile from Copeland Street, in the Boothen region of Stoke. The rather landlocked site originally abutted the former Newcastle-under-Lyme canal, now filled in, and was accessed off Summer Street. A new works was built, adjoining the original and this can be located by reference to the extracts from the Ordnance Survey of 1924 and 1937. Virtually nothing remains of this once thriving business, as the site, including the former Bilton's premises, is being developed for residential purposes. A few clues remain in the Street names and a forlorn fragment of the original entrance. Carlton's diversification into tea ware did not last long, as the combination of the fallout from the National Strike, and the loss of the export market following the American financial disaster, dealt a fatal blow. After just a few years of trading [1928-1933] a Receiver was appointed and Birks Rawlins and Co. Ltd. finally closed in about 1934.

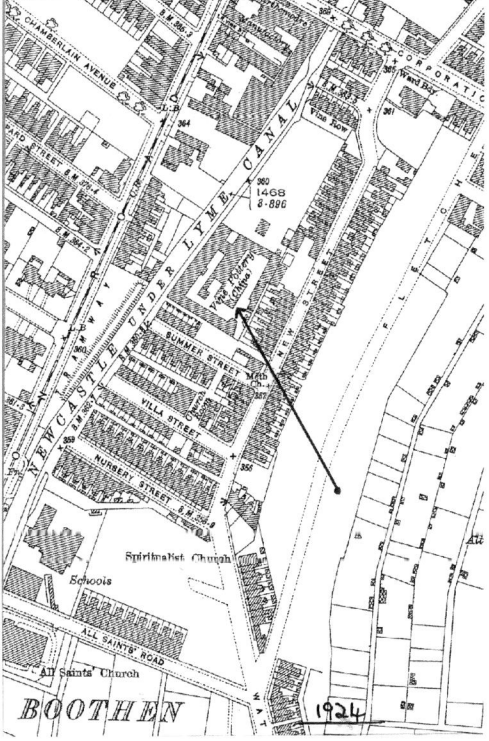

The Vine Pottery

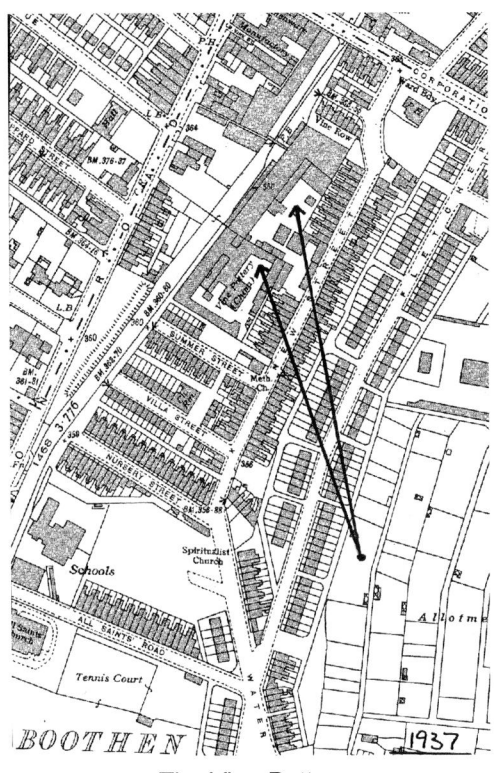
The Vine Pottery

The convention of taking tea is one of life's pleasures. This quintessentially English pastime could be enhanced by the use of a Carlton China tea service. The good quality ceramic was used to form feather light cups, saucers, tea and side plates, which were available in either circular or chamfered square form. Matching cake plates, coffee pots, creamers or sugar bowls [sucrieres] complemented the sets. Pedestal or Chinese shape cups with elaborate handles were also created. The ware was either transfer printed, freehand painted, or a combination of both. Top enamelling and gilding was added in considerable style.

Although the Carlton china patterns had a separate numbering system, this was not foolproof, as a few china items share numbers with their earthenware counterparts, particularly in the case of luxury vases. Wiltshaw and Robinson throughout their long history, produced many boxed coffee and tea services, but these were earthenware products.

Designs
Violet made her mark with the tea settings, the original purpose of her appointment. Her input was outstanding both in terms of quality and quantity. She contributed iconic designs, from delicate floral to a hint of art deco, each exuding a charm of its own. Her ideas were revolutionary when compared to the earlier, more traditional offerings of Birks Rawlins. It is quite likely that some of Miss Elmer's cherished designs were shown at the British Industries Fair at Olympia's Empire Hall in 1930.

Display of Carlton China

Violet's patterns depicted floral sprays, woodland scenes, fantasy birds and showed the influence of art deco. The ubiquitous **SUNSHINE** [4693], is an example of an earlier style, whilst **GARDEN** [4885], with its Q handle, has a more modern look and is worthy of special attention, owing to the exceptional hand applied detail and gold edging. Incidentally, the treatment of the delicate shrubs to be seen on Burleigh's Riviera are reminiscent of Carlton's own **GARDEN** design. The Carlton china format of sinuous trees, supplemented by shrubs and flowers, is demonstrated to good effect on **SPRINGTIME** [4754] and **Woodland** [4676]. Both of these designs echo the creativity of other factories. Shelley, with Balloon Tree, Royal Doulton with Eden and the Venton Pottery, with the Sunrise pattern. The **Woodland** pattern shows Miss Elmer's 'lollipop stick' trees, a stylised device that mirrors the work of Clarice Cliff, Burgess and Leigh and Royal Venton. **Sylvan Tree** [4986], a design reproduced on ware as pattern [3500], also follows this trait. Avian designs such as **Fantail Birds** [4864] and **Firecracker Tree** [4907] are masterful in their delicate use of colour and intricate design, with a minimum of hand painting to highlight the transfer print. **Firecracker Tree**, bears a resemblance to the earthenware **Explosion** pattern [3447] which was probably made earlier.

Some of the more radical later designs, verging on art deco, were extremely diverse but no less interesting. As can be seen from this final section, **Chinese Lanterns** [4906], was a combination of the traditional and the modern, and shared impact with Maling's Anzac. Inevitably the occasional design can be reflected in the product of more than one pottery. **Budeye** [4942] however, is truly individual and by its very nature can only be associated with Violet Elmer and Carlton China. The eclectic mix of components are fused together in an imaginative modern way. **Autumn Trees** [4998] is typical of the early 1930s, with the stylised landscape portrayed in vibrant colours. A final example from the Birks Rawlins era c.1932, was **Moon and House** [5001] unusually produced on a sponged light blue ground. Stylistically like Clarice Cliff, the indication of brush strokes confirms the paintresses' contribution to the charming scene.

SUNSHINE

GARDEN

SPRINGTIME

Woodland

Sylvan Tree

Fantail Birds

Chinese Lanterns

Budeye

Autumn Trees

Moon and House

Flirecracker Tree and Explosion

In 1932, Violet presented her friend Ruby, with a tea service on the occasion of her wedding. The service, **Clematis** [5000] was designed the same year and exists to this day. As well as being attributed to the artist, it was in all probability painted by Miss Elmer herself.

Clematis Tea Service

Product Range
The efforts of Violet and her assistants were commendable, especially given that they competed against the might of much larger concerns. Shelley Potteries with leading designer Eric Slater, J. Aynsley and Sons Limited, Foley China [E. Brain and Company Limited] and many others presented formidable opposition. Although the Carlton China operation only lasted a few years, it is believed that scores of new patterns were introduced, many of which are yet to be discovered.

Whilst some of the tea ware patterns go back as far as the 2000 numbering system, the majority, and probably most of Violet Elmer's designs are recorded by numbers in excess of 4500. Wiltshaw and Robinson's earlier, limited range of china tea wares carried a variant of the Crown Mark, but later a single script device was deemed sufficient. The Birks Rawlins brand name, 'Savoy China', was superceded by the 'Carlton China' label at the time of the takeover in 1928. Pattern books, representing the china company's product range still exist. It should be recorded that the 'Carlton China' back stamp was originally in use as long ago as 1902, to mark Carlton Heraldic [crested] china. During the 1930s, the pottery also produced attractive sets of bone china animals, especially of a canine variety, but these unfortunately did not bear a number. Contemporary with this, the company put their name to a series of china female figures predominantly in the pattern range 4260-4276.

The crossover of Violet's design's from tea ware, via Handcraft to Best Ware is intriguing. It would be a challenging exercise to precisely date an original image and then trace subsequent adaptation to other ware.

Chapter 9

Handcraft

Influence and Development

In 1928, and heralded as Handcraft, a new form of freehand experimental ware came into existence.

1929 Advertisement

It is likely that this new Carlton art form was initiated by Enoch Boulton but it is not possible to give credence to the assertion. Miss Elmer's arrival was imminent and no doubt there would be a considerable element of collaboration whilst Enoch remained at the factory. Following this, it would be Violet who would make a brave statement with this new design style. A palette of just a few colours was used on the early examples of this matt glazed, less ornate marque of Handcraft, although later examples were more flamboyant. This was a most interesting period in the life of the manufactory. The studio pottery appearance uniquely elevated the brand, which would remain a viable product for several years. Something different was certainly needed and Violet Elmer would soon find herself involved. These inexpensively made goods were introduced following the success of A. J. Wilkinson, with Clarice Cliff's interpretation of the new style. The Poole and Dutch designers, amongst others, also influenced Carlton Ware at this time. The decorating concern of A. E. Gray Limited had several well known designers in its ranks, including Susie Cooper, and was another market leader. These hand painted floral and geometric designs in the art deco style would not have gone unnoticed by the Carlton Ware art department. The new range was the antithesis of the heavily decorated chinoiserie and fantasy bird designs. The character of these new Carlton art pottery products caught the imagination with their improved modern design. Early Handcraft examples include, **BUTTERFLY** [3290], **HAREBELL** [3294] and were designed by Violet in her first years at the factory c.1928–29.

BUTTERFLY

Additional early Dutch inspired variants from about 1929 included **Florabunda** [3236], **Flowering Papyrus** [3242] and **DUTCH** [3250]. More colourful floral versions followed

HAREBELL

Table Lamp in DUTCH design

Gentian

in the form of **Gentian** [3358] c.1930, **Peach Melba** [3448] c.1931, **CLEMATIS** [3525] c.1932 and **PRIMULA** [3745] c.1934. However, considerable advancement was made

Farrago

with the creation of a new generation of designs, such as **Farrago** [3297] c.1929 and **Carnival** [3305] c.1930. These modern interpretations may well have influenced Enoch Boulton's thinking in the creation of the **JAZZ** [3352] design. Such modern elements were later to be found in some of the Best Ware products. The pinnacle of Handcraft achievement was attained during the next few years with such stunning examples as **SCROLL** [3411], **Geometrica** [3566], **RUSSIAN** [3567], and in 1933 **Intersection** [3690]. These were vibrant designs ahead of their time, many of which, by reference to the sequencing of pattern numbers, could be attributed to Miss Elmer's prolific output. Caution is needed regarding the validation of new patterns; for instance the Handcraft **CLEMATIS** [3525] appeared at about the same time on a Carlton China tea service. On occasion, the same design was also used on both tea ware and Best Ware products. Difficulty is compounded by ambiguity in the marking of some Handcraft pieces. This point is borne out by a group of stylish art deco designs produced by Violet c.1932 and unusually branded as Handcraft. The best of these, namely **Eclipse** [3551], **Deco Fan** [3552], **Strata** [3553] and **Ziggurat** [3554] only appear to have been applied to coffee sets.

SCROLL

RUSSIAN

Chapter 10

Carlton Ware and Crown Devon

Similarity, Rivalry and the Jazz Pattern
Over the forthcoming years, there was a marked likeness of design between the ornamental ware of the two factories, including such items as coffee sets. There existed a proclivity for bird patterns, with sometimes, just a small difference between respective elements. The conspicuous similarity of Violet Elmer's **Fantasia** [3388] design and Enoch Boulton's almost identical Fantazia is such an example. Elements from both patterns appear to originate from a plate by Harry Clarke for an edition of Hans Christian Anderson's Fairy Tales. The significant difference is the interpretation by the two respective artists of the fantasy bird. Whereas Boulton's portrayal is more true to the original and includes the moon, Elmer's enjoys greater licence. The matter is perhaps best left unresolved.

On occasion the same shape has been used with a minor adjustment. A Carlton Ware flared Velox bowl, 10″ in diameter and 6″ in height only differs from a version by Fieldings in the design of the feet. The Carlton Ware bowl is supported on three ball feet, whereas Fielding's bowl has the three ball feet enlarged by an art deco appendage. Some of the Crown Devon designs of the 1930s also feature floral devices not unlike those seen in many of the best products from Copeland Street.

Although Enoch's early work at the Devon Pottery bore the stamp of Wiltshaw and Robinson, subsequent developments such as the renowned Mattajade were more individual and unique. The rivalry between both Works during the 1930s would be intense, sparking off wonderful earthenware products, with Enoch for Fieldings and Violet for Carlton Ware. Judgemental comparison is unnecessary, for, if either were superior it would be in the eye of the beholder. The competition progressively extended the ability of these talented individuals to achieve such excellence. Following success with oriental designs, **TUTANKHAMEN** [2711] and **CHINALAND** [3015] it was the inception of **JAZZ** attributed in 1929 shortly before

JAZZ Pattern No. 3352

leaving, that would be Enoch Boulton's crowning glory. This art deco design which encapsulated the times, announced the company's entry into arguably the greatest period of its history. This design alone would inspire the young nascent Violet Elmer to ever greater heights in the forthcoming years. Even though Enoch and Violet worked simultaneously at the Carlton Works it must be conjecture whether during this brief time, there was any collaboration. Inevitably some of Enoch's ideas and work would have been lost to Carlton Ware in his transfer to Fieldings. Although there may be a difficulty of pattern attribution at this time, it is beyond doubt that their respective abilities were unquestionable.

Chapter 11

Violet Elmer Designer 1928-1938

Change of Environment
In 1928 the twenty-one year old Miss Elmer left home. What a contrast it must have been, exchanging the classical elegance of her home city, just a short walk along Abingdon Road and over Folly Bridge, for the industrial activity of Stoke-on-Trent. In those

Glebe Street, Stoke-upon-Trent

days The Potteries would not have been a very healthy environment in which to work and live, with life expectancy less than the average. During the late 1920s the inhabitants of Stoke-on-Trent existed cheek by jowl with a plethora of coal-fired bottle ovens. It would not be until the mid 1950s that an almost miraculous improvement would be achieved in relation to smoke pollution. This was brought about by a combination of the Clean Air Act, together with the use of gas and electricity to fire the kilns. Unlike today, many individual stores and shops were trading in Stoke and motor car ownership was still a preserve of the wealthy. Public transport however, would have been available to convey the young Miss Elmer from Newcastle to the factory a few miles away.

Liverpool Road, Stoke-upon-Trent

This was the time when Violet would first have been able to vote, as all women over 21 had, after a long struggle, obtained equal suffrage. A decade earlier, women over thirty had the right but this was conditional. The country was becoming more liberated, after years of male domination.

It was only in 1925 that Stoke-on-Trent had acquired city status. Earlier, in 1910, the six towns of Burslem, Fenton, Hanley, Longton, Stoke-upon-Trent and Tunstall had been confederated into the county borough of Stoke-on-Trent. During the 1920s and 30s and even later, the city made several unsuccessful attempts to take over Violet's adopted home town of Newcastle-under-Lyme.

As is known, Violet was appointed to design the new Carlton china products and she soon became involved, as will be seen, in other areas of production, rapidly making her mark. The company was entering into one of the most turbulent and transitional stages in its long history but it was undeniably exciting. There was more to follow - much more ....

Despite unhelpful trading conditions in the early 1930s, and the danger of closure, the company managed to turn adversity into triumph. A new wave of ceramics was conceived, the quality and design of which would not be exceeded. The products revealed during this decade, in terms of creativity and workmanship, would prove to be of a golden age. Good management, a skilled workforce, and most importantly the design team, drove the Copeland Street Works forward. The accomplished Miss Elmer had posted a declaration of intent. After the early difficulty, the 1930s were witness to the continuation of the prolific output of both commercial and luxury goods. In 1929 the company made a major decision to allow Violet the chance to succeed Enoch Boulton as principal designer. After only a relatively short time spent at the factory, it was perhaps surprising that she was given this opportunity. Her artistic ability, at such an extremely young age, had not gone unnoticed. The recognition of her early imaginative accomplishments by such a forward thinking management, helped to propel the Carlton Works on to even greater achievements.

Lodgings

Upon her move to The Potteries, Violet had taken up lodgings in a large Victorian house built c.1895 in Friars Wood Road [now known as Friarswood Road] adjacent to the Lyme Valley Brook, Newcastle-under-Lyme. She probably resided there throughout the time she was employed by Wiltshaw and Robinson. The property is located about two miles from the factory at Stoke-on-Trent and within half a mile from her final home at Westlands. The

Friarswood Road, Newcastle-under-Lyme

property had occupants of some interest. In 1933 the owner is listed as Maria, [known as Bia], Scott, who was familiar with the Arts and had connections in the Industry. Also living at the premises was one Albert Simmonds, a relative of Bia. Aside from Violet, the remaining occupant was designer Olive Kew. The 1933 Electoral Register, for the period 15th October 1933 – 14th October 1934, includes the names of all persons eligible to vote. The Register states that both Maria and Albert lived and worked in Newcastle and that Violet and Olive lived in Newcastle, but neither worked there.

Should the young designers' social life have embraced the world of cinema they would have witnessed Gracie Fields in her hey day with George Formby waiting in the wings.

Floral Embossed – The Influence of Violet Elmer
Production of established decorative and tableware items from the previous decade would continue throughout the 1930s, allied to many new products. An early development associated with Miss Elmer was Cottage Ware. Products included a biscuit barrel, modelled as a thatched cottage, with walls featuring simulated brickwork and garden hedges, a preserve pot in the form of a circular cottage and a toast rack featuring a dwelling at either end, subdivided by a five barred gate. The cottages had cream or yellow walls; brown thatched or red tile roofs and were adorned with delightful doors and windows. The young artist's trade mark trees and shrubs could also be seen. Cottage Ware was available in strong colours with a gloss finish.

The archetypal floral and fruit embossed ware with its origins in the 1930s was the product which most closely symbolised the company. This everyday domestic group, appealingly modelled in relief, enhanced with embossed flowers and fruit, came predominantly in soft ground colours of green, lemon and pink. Jugs with handles in the form of a branch or flower stem, replete with the addition of a bud or floral device delighted the eye. Carlton Ware had achieved an enviable up-dating of early English naturalistic designs previously pioneered by Thomas Whieldon,

Josiah Wedgwood and the Chelsea and Longton Hall factories. The format can also be seen in the products of Royal Doulton and the County Fermanagh Pottery of Belleek. Although there was competition from the fertile minds of Beswick by way of their large range of salad ware, together with Fielding's Crown Devon, Royal Winton and Shorter and Son, the elegant modern interpretation achieved at Carlton Ware was unsurpassed. The concept of the embossed ware inevitably bears the hand of such visionary designers as Violet Elmer between the years 1932-1938 and thereafter the challenge was accepted by Irene Pemberton.

One of the first floral embossed patterns to be produced from about 1934 was Anemone, which was available for several years and usually found in a deep yellow, of moulded shape, with leaves and flower heads in orange and burgundy. Some ranges might be discontinued and re-introduced at a much later date. Generally the original pieces would be found to be more detailed and of a higher quality. This ware is sometimes known as the "Australian Design" because of the difficulty that many English potteries experienced owing to the copying of designs by Japanese manufacturers, with consequent loss of sales. Around 1937 to combat this export problem, and afford an element of protection, the Australian authorities enabled an easier design registration and consequent backstamp. The pottery's logo in this respect was "Carlton Ware, Made in England, "Trade Mark" Registered Australian Design, Registration Applied For". It should be noted that at no time were the products manufactured other than at the Stoke-on-Trent factory.

Many were the varied designs and shapes devised during the second half of the 1930s, resulting in a prodigious output from the factory. It should be borne in mind that this was only part of the company's total production. The popular new floral embossed designs provided a much needed stimulus to the development of the earthenware enterprise. Some of these moulded products were reminiscent of the Rococo style. Floral decoration in the form of sprigs could be added, and once the ground colour had been applied by the aerographer, the relief decoration was completed by the underglaze paintress. As usual, the subject poses difficulty in the precise dating of ware, attribution of designers and many other aspects. There will be a considerable amount of ink spilt before the full story is known.

At about the same time as Anemone, a fundamentally different naturalistic design known as Oak was created. The embossed design comprised a stylised oak tree with foliage. Two colour combinations dominate, a blue ground with beige detail and a buff ground with green and yellow elements. During 1933 to 1935 the company produced the stoneware range of vases and jugs, unadorned but aesthetically pleasing, in subdued colours with a soft ribbed exterior surface. Oak shares the same characteristic of that hand potted style. A large stoneware vase and Oak jug share the same body, with minor adjustments. There are other examples of the same mould being used for different products. The configuration of the tree on an Oak charger resembles that found on an unnumbered Best Ware example, a dual use, perhaps, of a Violet Elmer image. There is evidence of patterns, or sections thereof, being used on other factory products, perhaps a study in itself. The stoneware product [old stoneware] should not be confused with Carlton's engine-turned pieces produced about the same time. These plain pastel objects, in the manner of Keith Murray for Wedgwood, are marked with incised annular rings, a product way ahead of its time.

Old Stoneware

New embossed patterns were now appearing in rapid succession, both Fruit Basket and Rock Garden being offered about 1935. The former included highly glazed tableware, such as jugs on a vivid green, or bright yellow ground, and toast racks all exhibiting different varieties of fruit. The pyramidical arrangement of fruit on the sugar shaker was a particular joy. Rock Garden was different and more for decorative use than the practical. Each item, whether, for instance, a vase or charger, was moulded in similar form, the body being subdivided into imitation brickwork and

Rock Garden

horizontal banding. Jugs were finished with rope effect handles. The moulded brick effect was encrusted with an array of cottage flowers. This attractive understated design was available in various pastel shades including green, lemon and celadon.

The versatility of the factory was most apparent in Buttercup, one of the best floral embossed designs ever produced by Wiltshaw and Robinson. The art work was drawn from a close observation of nature. Marketed about 1935, and in all probability from the portfolio of Miss Elmer, the ware was produced in a choice of either yellow or pink. However, although a hybrid and more difficult to find, it is the pink ground pieces that are particularly coveted. The ceramic is moulded in the shape of overlapping petals and detailed by carpel and stamen. Elements of the flower were also used in an enterprising manner to form handles and spouts. Sugar shakers, teapots, cheese dishes and general tableware items were produced in varying sizes as well as boxed sets such as salad bowls with serving spoon and fork. These attractive gift-sets are often to be found unused to this day. It was the success of Buttercup that was instrumental in restoring the fortunes of the company.

The Tulip design which came of age c.1937 was another concept during Miss Elmer's reign. The strong glaze finish of the cream coloured moulded body, together with colourful flower heads, was reminiscent of the earlier Orange Ware. Stylish and understated, cruets, jugs and biscuit barrels were distinctly art deco in style. Owing to the paucity of pieces, the challenge of starting a collection of Tulip will require perseverance. Embossed patterns continued to appear with great regularity and also c.1937, the company sanctioned the release of Wild Rose, a tableware line of typically moulded pieces, which would confirm the factory as a market leader. The teapot was particularly attractive; a moulded striated body with raised green leaves and pink flowers and the lid embellished with a rosebud finial. Wild Rose came in either a green or yellow ground, the jugs being fitted with naturalistic brown handles. All the embossed patterns were well modelled and painted by hand. It is possible that Wild Rose may have been one of Violet Elmer's last floral embossed designs. It was important that original moulds were regularly replaced, as owing to continual heavy usage, sharpness of detail would eventually become lost. This is borne out in a series of the factory named 'beaker and covers' more commonly known as chocolate mugs, where the detail of some vary considerably. A few of the floral embossed ranges from the 1930s are depicted in the form of the well crafted mugs shown. These include Apple Blossom, Buttercup, Foxglove, Springtime and Water Lily. Notice the delightful floral handles including that of the contemporary musical tankard.

In 1938, René Pemberton took over and would return after the war. Although the joint design influence was all pervasive, attribution of patterns during this handover period, again poses some difficulty. Some of Violet Elmer's ideas could have been taken forward by others after her departure, although it must not be forgotten that Miss Pemberton possessed her own fine body of work. Caution should also be exercised regarding the fruit and floral embossed products detailed, as this catalogue does not purport to be comprehensive. However, during the period 1936-1940, other embossed patterns such as Blackberry, Raspberry and Redcurrant came to fruition at the Carlton Works whilst the flowers of the Apple, Poppy and Water Lily also enabled the works to blossom. The enlightened decision by the directors of Wiltshaw and Robinson to invite the seminal artist to join the company can only be

Floral Embossed

described as inspired, as the faith shown proved to be a sound investment. It was a travesty that company policy precluded the designers marking their own ceramics; nonetheless, individual characteristics prevail over anonymity.

The Wedding of Ruby Moss

Proceedings were briefly interrupted at this time in that Violet's childhood friend, Ruby Moss, was to marry. The designer left her lodgings at Newcastle-under-Lyme and returned home for the special occasion. On the 2nd April 1932, Ruby married Arthur Russell of Oxford at St Matthews Church, Grandpont, the same

Ruby's Wedding

Entering the Church

parish church in which a few years later Violet herself would take her wedding vows. The photograph recalls the special day in twenty five year old Ruby's life. Standing beside her, Violet can be seen as chief bridesmaid. The beautiful skullcaps were designed and made by the bride and in all probability, her veil and the bridesmaids' dresses. One bridesmaid can still recall the special event and that the colour of her dress was gold. Miss Elmer was also an official witness to the ceremony, which was taken by the long serving Reverend David Stather-Hunt, vicar of St Matthews 1929-1975. He would preside at Violet's wedding a few years later.

Upon her return to the factory, following the visit to her home city, the conceptual artist, would, with renewed zeal, continue to apply herself to the progressively extensive Wiltshaw and Robinson product range.

Introduction to Art Deco and Best Ware
A portent of the future was to be found in Miss Elmer's intricate tea ware patterns, valued Handcraft input, and embossed undertaking.

JAZZ on shape 442

This was the ideal preparation, if any were needed, for the application of her skills to the design of the pottery's ultimate, or second-generation, best earthenware products. Although the embossed ware, which was marketed over several decades, was the lifeblood of the company, the high point of design and realisation of the skills of the workforce was to be seen in Best Ware. The ultimate luxury brand was produced at considerable expense, from its inception in 1929, to the outset of the Second World War. Following the lead given by Enoch Boulton's **JAZZ** design this was the perfect time and environment for the flourishing of Miss Elmer's talents. An abundance of influences, a supportive management, a bank of skills that would not be surpassed, welcomed the burgeoning artist to centre stage. In view of the complexity of some of the new order designs, it is surprising that she was able simultaneously to devote time to other factory products.

More generally, an element of confusion exists, concerning products from some of the Staffordshire potters which bear a resemblance to one another. Which designer at which factory was the originator of a new concept and which other potteries exploited the idea? A not unfamiliar circumstance with obvious commercial implications.

The art deco trend, once up and running in The Potteries, was no doubt all pervasive and it must have been impossible for the enthusiastic designer not to notice what was going on around her. Although her classic art deco and fantasy designs are outstanding, there is evidence as has been seen, in some of the tea ware designs, of a similarity of form and components to products of other manufacturers. This is inevitable in view of the large output of art deco tea ware from many of the Staffordshire potters at the time.

No doubt an across the board comparison of pottery designs during this period would reveal quite interesting results. The late 1920s and early 1930s must have been such exciting times for the well known manufacturers engaged in the art deco movement. The dilemma of attribution within the crossover period of the late 1920s between Boulton and Elmer alone might never be fully resolved. What is not in doubt is that they both continued individually to achieve a reputation for work of the highest order. There were also outside influences to be seen in the stylised art work of Poole, Grays, New Pearl and Royal Winton amongst others. Although the source of inspiration may be elusive, clues do exist. For instance, elements from the Delft 'handcraft like' Poole palette, applied at the time on a white ground, would have been

Carnival

familiar to Violet. If Carlton's **Carnival** [3305] pattern resembled the work of the Poole potters, it could only be seen as an acknowledgement to the prowess of the eminent Truda Carter and her colleagues. The use of small sub-design insignia can sometimes be traced from one designer to another and this is so with regard to the trumpet shape flowers found on the **Rainbow Fan** [3700] and also the Carlton china **Flower and Cloud** [4989]. Thought to be of French origin, the concept was taken up by Truda Carter and at a later date seems to have been incorporated by Miss Elmer in one of her designs. With such a plethora of radical material available, together with adaptations and refinements of original themes, the achievement of true originality would not have been easy. Art Deco is thematic, with essential recurring characteristics, combined with a stylistic approach to nature, architecture and transport.

Violet would rise to the challenge and at the peak of her powers, during the early to late 1930s create a catalogue of work, the equal of any other designer. In the world of ceramics Violet Irene Ellen Elmer, late of Oxford, would come of age.

Identification of Violet Elmer's Work

The need to identify the artist's work is essential and there exist several methods of doing this, some distinctly more accurate than others. It is a pity though that this exercise is hindered by the lack of factory records and availability of information. There are positives, in that Wiltshaw and Robinson were generous in the marking of their products, by the provision of a range of backstamps and symbols on the base of their ceramics. From the base of the Best Ware vase shown, the standard "Carlton Ware" script trade mark can clearly be seen. Centre right is the prefixed

Backstamp Lacecap Hydrangea

four digit order or batch number, in this case 1/8067. Beneath this is the four digit pattern number 3969 which, in this instance, relates to **Lacecap Hydrangea**. Uppermost is the impress mark 1232 E, the indentation which relates to the shape of the vase. The remaining small characters have been applied by the gilder and the paintress.

Although of interest, certain methods can be dismissed as being of little value as it is first necessary to establish the date of a design and then relate this to Violet's tenure at the factory. Curiosity abounds concerning the Copeland Street enterprise and in particular with regard to the prefixed four digit number to be found on the base of the Best Ware products of the 1920s and 30s. This order or batch number would no doubt have related to retail outlets and the placement of an order but this cannot be tested for veracity. From its early leaning purely towards Wiltshaw and Robinson, the company's backstamp changed many times to embrace such products as Carlton China, Carlton Armand, Handcraft and the Rouge brands. "Carlton Ware", as a logo, was incorporated in the Crown mark, depicting a swallow, long ago.

During Miss Elmer's time, the ubiquitous Carlton script mark would have been in use. Introduced c.1926, this mark was displayed on the company's artefacts for several decades, and consequently is of little value in the procedure.

Although they can be discounted in terms of a dating mechanism, the small symbols to be found on the underside of a Carlton Best Ware ceramic are worthy of attention. These individual letters or numerals performed an important function and were applied by the freehand paintresses, enamellers or gilders. They would have been paid at different rates, in view of their respective skills. The enameller would paint within a given parameter whereas the paintress would have considerable licence of interpretation.

The company took considerable time to train their fledgling apprentices, who were schooled in the decorating department, on a training plate until competent. These employees were invariably retained on a piecework basis and their personal mark allowed identification of their work. This enabled the weekly calculation of wages, subject to the work being satisfactory. The person in charge of the decorating process, usually a woman, was traditionally described as a "Missus", an experienced senior paintress or enameller. Apart from training and supervision and the maintaining of high decorative standards, it was the "Missus" who did the settling; that is, the working out of the paintresses' weekly wages.

The long-term loyalty of staff was reflected in the way that the same marks could be found recurring over many years. As for ownership of a particular device, that is another matter, for as considerable time had now elapsed since the heyday of the 1930s, accreditation of work is exceedingly difficult. However, the interpretation of Violet Elmer's complex designs, deserved to be well rewarded.

In addition to the personal characters, there was also to be found, adjoining the backstamp, the registration number. Under Parliamentary Law, the purpose of the Act was to afford protection to new designs and deter copying. Many factory pieces were stamped with a registration number from the beginning of the business in 1890 to the late 1920s. Unfortunately, its usage declined, and it is not to be found on products of the second-generation Best Ware era. A further opportunity to establish a design date is by resort to the impress or shape number to be found as an indentation on the base of the ware. This number defined the shape of the ceramic, and when it was originally potted according to the table of numbers. Impress numbers in the low one hundreds are not uncommon but generally the shape numbers allotted to Miss Elmer's Best Ware designs fall between numbers 200 and 800 with the majority in the 400 series. However, this again is an imprecise method, as the same shape, probably even in differing sizes, would retain its original number when used over a span of several years. Any notion of a foolproof system can again be quickly dispelled.

Identification of the floral embossed designs relies heavily on their own impress numbers, as unlike Best Ware patterns, individual pattern numbers were not applied. By reference to such shape books that do exist, these numbers can be used to obtain the date a particular embossed shape was first introduced.

The focus now turns to the last remaining symbol contained on the Carlton Ware product, which affords the best opportunity of dating and therefore a more accurate attribution of Violet's work. This is the four-digit pattern number, which is to be found on all Wiltshaw and Robinson's Best Ware products and without which so little would be known. The system seemingly commenced with zero at the birth of the factory and had reached in excess of pattern number 4000 by the outbreak of the Second World War. There appears to have been an approximate allocation of a hundred numbers per year. Most of the designs known today were named either by the factory - a surprisingly small number - or at a later date by relevant club enthusiasts.

For whatever reason, the pottery did not include either the pattern name or designer's name on their products. Despite the lack of a more inspired treatise, at the time of Violet's arrival at Copeland Street in 1928, it is calculated that Best Ware pattern numbers would have been in the order of 3100-3200. Projecting the formula to 1938, at which time she ceased her labours, the pattern numbers would be in the order of 4100-4200. It should be remembered that the specific number would indicate the year the design was first produced.

As the application of Violet Elmer's skills to Best Ware would not have been immediate, it is probable that her creativity would be represented between patterns numbered 3200-4200. Conceivably, as the prolific designer married mid 1938, it is also unlikely that there would be many attributions that particular year. Conversely, it is also possible that some of her designs may have been produced after her departure. Therefore, in conclusion, there is every prospect that her designs would fall within the foregoing pattern range. Violet's designs can also be dated with reasonable certainty to a particular year in view of the exceedingly small production runs of the time.

Care should be exercised as anomalies do exist such as the **JAZZ** designs of Enoch Boulton, pattern numbers 3352, 3353 and 3361 which indicate perhaps a slightly later date than 1929 when he resigned from the company. Again, it may be that some of his work was not released until after he had left Copeland Street. As another example, the dating of Irene Pemberton's popular **SPIDERS WEB** [4244] would be more problematic. First offered c.1938 and produced for many years thereafter, precise dating of an individual piece would be speculative. It should be recorded that the Handcraft products were included in the system but not the everyday commercial items. The tea ware also partook of a separate arrangement more to its own taste.

SPIDERS WEB dish

There may well be other irregularities yet to reveal themselves. On occasion a previously unknown pattern will come to light, quite often devoid of pattern number, order number and impress mark. Such an occurrence is not unique but does add excitement to the

Stardust charger

pursuit. The type of backstamp alone will not be sufficient to enable precise dating or attribution and additional progress can only be made by recognition of the designer's characteristics. The two splendid unmarked chargers shown, which have recently been discovered, are probably prototypes that did not go into production. The stylised tree and bejewelled canopy of **Stardust** and the phoenix-like bird of the other, give every indication of a Violet association. Also shown is a tray in **PERSIAN ROSE**, again unmarked, and thought to be the only representation of this pattern in a blue colourway. Chargers offered the best prospect of fully displaying a pattern and featured designs from the Best Ware, floral embossed, and Handcraft period. They came in two sizes, either slightly in excess of 12" or 15". Only relatively few designs were used in this format, some in a matt finish, others in lustre.

Phoenix charger

All, such as the embossed Rock Garden, the floral **ANEMONE** [3694] and **Summer Medley** [3663] presented well. However, it is the art deco **BELL** [3786 green], **Egyptian Fan** [3696 blue] and **Floral Comet** [3422

PERSIAN ROSE tray

blue] together with the Handcraft **RUSSIAN** [3567] that are the best of all. A reference to **VICTORIAN LADY** [3451] is also justified as this demonstrates the licence given to the Carlton Ware paintresses. There are two versions of this charger, one having a larger main figure. However, even chargers bearing the same crinoline lady are not identical as subtle nuances define originality. For instance, the cloud formation, shadow effect, shrubs and trees vary from one example to another.

From the evidence available, the dating of Violet's designs has been determined with reasonable certainty but the information given does not purport to be definitive. The same problems apply to the attribution of her work as to that of the other Carlton Ware designers.

ANEMONE

Summer Medley

VICTORIAN LADY

Chapter 12

Olive Kew Designer 1930-1931

Following a recommendation by a family member, who was a friend of Mr L. O. Smith, a manager at the pottery, Olive began work at Carlton Ware as a design assistant to Miss Elmer in February 1930. At Copeland Street, they shared a 'long narrow office' and became great friends. However, sadly, the situation would not last. In March 1931, Olive's services had to be terminated as the company was facing receivership and it could no longer afford the luxury of two full time designers.

Once again, owing to the lack of records, together with the passage of time, it is difficult to establish with any certainty, attribution of Miss Kew's work. However, it is thought that **Jagged Bouquet** [3457] should be accredited. Other designs must surely exist and a case for **Prickly Pansy** [3449], and **Towering Castle** [3458], both of which show similarities and fall within the same numbering range, could perhaps be made.

Prickly Pansy   Jagged Bouquet

Later that year [1931] after leaving Carlton Ware, she joined the Howard Pottery, Shelton, Stoke-on-Trent, the maker of Brentleigh Ware. This was mostly cellulose decorated. There, Olive enjoyed considerable success as a designer and stayed until 1957.

She remained in employment within The Potteries until retirement in 1962, working at Kirkhams, London Road, Stoke-on-Trent, where she was not very happy. Miss Kew was probably also employed by Shaw and Copestake, Longton, manufactures of the 'SylvaC' brand.

There is no doubt that Olive Kew was a talented designer who served several companies with distinction. Unfortunately much of her work remains unrecorded. The photographs show Miss Kew at different times in her life. The two Carlton Ware designers can be

Chapter 14

Christopher Boulton Designer c.1952-1954

A unique image of a designer at work is shown in a film shot at the factory in 1952 entitled "Pottery for the Modern Age". The designer is also seen perusing some drawings, which include the floral embossed Hydrangea, as well as the Pemberton attributed **New Stork** [4280] and **SPIDERS WEB**. A few more, depicted vases whose form exceeded their decoration. Of studio-like appearance one had a minimum of gilt lining and another was in the art nouveau style. It is odd that they bear pattern numbers of a decade earlier, however this could be explained by the curtailment of production [and decoration] owing to the government restrictions of World War Two.

The film also shows a glittering array of ware on display at the firms Copeland Street showroom and is an indicator of the company's fortunes at the time. It could be seen that although chinoiserie still dominated, more modern products like elegant spiral ginger jars were available. Other ornamentals on view included **LILY OF THE VALLEY** [4488], **VINE** [4385] and the aforementioned **New Stork** and **SPIDERS WEB**. The embossed range was represented by Foxglove, Hydrangea and Vine [sometimes known as Grape].

John Christopher Boulton

The designer who is seen in the film seated at his drawing board, so precisely outlining a covered vase is Christopher Boulton. Although slowed by a lost generation and the blurred memories of the contemporaries that remain, good fortune can sometimes occur. In this instance, a debt is owed to Christopher's surviving sister for corroboration and additional facts. Christopher Boulton could have been the successor to designer Irene Pemberton after she retired in 1949. As yet, precise details of his service are unclear although he was proven to still be at Copeland Street in 1954. Specific attribution may be unwise but it is likely that some of his work is reflected in the drawings and showroom pieces preserved for posterity on the celluloid of some sixty years ago.

Christopher had an eventful life, he was employed as a designer at Price Bros. [Burslem] Ltd., earthenware manufacturers from 1927 to the outbreak of war and briefly afterwards. Following employment at Leek, he returned to The Potteries and joined Wiltshaw and Robinson as a designer. On leaving Carlton Ware, he joined Spode. Whilst there, in 1963, he was invited by Harold Holdway to design a plate based on the Book of Kells. Boulton's 'Iona' plate was well received and inspired Holdway himself to even greater success with a series of commemorative patterns. It was in 1934, that Holdway joined the Spode works of W.T. Copeland and Sons as a designer. He then proceeded to attain the position of chief designer and head of the decorating department before eventually becoming a director. During his lifetime he created many highly successful designs.

Bridal Rose plate

Iona plate

Loving Cup

Some of Christopher Boulton's other designs for Spode included "Bridal Rose", and the fine draughtsmanship of nativity scenes. He finished his career at Coalport where he designed a loving cup to commemorate the Queen's Silver jubilee. Some additional information regarding the life of the designer can be found by reference to Chapter 19.

Chapter 15

Best Ware Designs 1930 -1938

Designs 1930

Although her presence was in demand elsewhere in the design department, Miss Elmer was now about to embark on what would prove to be the most illustrious phase of her career. Many were the exotic, art deco and fantasy designs, which were to flow from her pen in the ensuing years. These were to adorn the manufacture of the company's earthenware products such as ginger jars, vases, chargers, tea and coffee services. As her output during the forthcoming period would have resulted in a design catalogue the equal of any other, it is a matter of concern that Violet Elmer has remained anonymous for so long. Most of the patterns were complex, intricate and therefore time consuming and expensive to manufacture. It is unfortunate that Carlton's Best Ware did not form a more individual marque with a separate branding of its own.

ZIG ZAG

Some of Miss Elmer's earliest pieces made their début c.1930, the first proper evidence being found in a selection which included **ZIG ZAG** [3299], **Floral Comet** [3387] and **Fantasia** [3388]. **ZIG ZAG** is included here as it is a printed example rather than a freehand painted 'handcraft' piece. Categorising some patterns continues to present problems and there is a definite similarity between **ZIG ZAG** and the Handcraft **Lightning** together with **Chevron** [3657] which appeared a few years later. Shown, is a fine **ZIG ZAG** velox bowl in a colourway of cream, orange and black and its counterpart **Lightning** [3356] in two tone blue. **Floral Comet** is a combination of lightning flashes, together with a stylised floral motif with a gilt print outline. Elements as varied as blue leaves on a brown and yellow mottled backdrop reveal

Lightning

a surprisingly harmonious outcome. With the unusual brown interior, set off by a delicate frieze, such a vase, containing seemingly such diverse elements, presents a most striking effect. There followed other variants, 3405, and 3422 usually seen on a ground colour of blue, with finishes such as a matt glaze, lustre, or a combination of the two. As stated, a different pattern number would be allocated to each colourway. One of the most fascinating aspects of Miss Elmer's work was the use of colour, and the dichotomy of design resulting from the placing of modern components with traditional themes, together with a combination of colours that appear incompatible with one another. The vibrancy of her creations is proof of a successful adjustment of the parameters - shades perhaps of Leon Bakst, the Russian painter, and designer of costumes and sets for the Ballets Russes.

The innovative application of the transfer gilt print to **Floral Comet** deserves attention. On one side it is applied upwards from the foot of the vase, and on the reverse downwards from the top. Signs of the paintress's brush are also visible. Patterns or parts thereof were used in an imaginative way to fit a particular shape. Elements of one pattern were sometimes included in another.

Floral Comet on green

Floral Comet on blue

Fantasia [3388]

As previously mentioned, **Fantasia** accredited to Miss Elmer, closely resembles a similar product of the Crown Devon Pottery which welcomed Enoch Boulton to its ranks in 1929/30. This may have been the result of a symbiotic relationship. The Carlton Ware version, features a typical Violet Elmer canopy. The main pattern, being formed by stylised polychrome trees, tracery and seed heads, is exhibited to good effect on an 8″ vase. The eye-catching swallow-type birds, together with wonderful under and overglaze work to the foot, are compelling features. All the agents of decoration are to be seen: lithographic work, gilt transfer, hand painting of shadows and considerable onglaze enamelling, in the form of a myriad of minute flowers and beading. The vase is finished in a matt light blue glaze with frieze and pink interior. Examples of this pattern in powder blue lustre, with onglaze enamelling and gilding are also to be found, namely pattern 3421. As Miss Elmer's watercolours were influenced by artists of the day, so it was with **Fantasia**, bearing as it does a close resemblance to well known illustrators of the time.

Designs 1931
Two fine art deco examples arrived in that year. **Awakening** [3453] and **Explosion** [3447], both being appropriately named. The matt green **Awakening** as shown, comprises a mixture of the abstract and art deco, a decorative tour de force.

A radiant sun is seen rising over a rural scene accompanied by fantasy shards of light and framed by an outline of clouds. The image of the sun is encased in a 'burning headdress' of colour as it illuminates the landscape. The detail of the individual design segments helps to create the dazzling display. A large spectrum of colour was used, ranging from the unusual to the more familiar. The use of cobalt blue and orange is softened by those pigments

Awakening

more mellow. The green 'melon like' ground is an excellent foil for the intricate arrangement. The interior of the **Awakening** ginger jar is plain white. The design fits the 8" product perfectly and is repeated to good effect both on the reverse and also on the cover.

Explosion

The **Explosion** pattern was produced in both a lustre and a matt finish. The name more than adequately describes the eye-catching ornament which can be seen on a 6" matt blue colourway [3447]. The interior is finished in black. It is a striking and inventive pattern. The mottled ground of duck egg blue is beset with a black star outlined in gilt, which in turn is overlaid on a framework of dark blue with copious tracery. The decorative circles, some of which have a shadow, refine the design. There is very little overglaze hand painting, just a spot of pink to lift the central design and a few touches to an itinerant butterfly. Once again, the design is found in a condensed, but no less attractive form on the reverse of the vase. On the matt ground, this is a sophisticated offering from Copeland Street. As has been seen a common theme exists between the **Explosion** pattern and the tea ware **Firecracker Tree** [4907].

Designs 1932

Suitably refreshed from participating at her friend Ruby's wedding in her home city of Oxford, Violet produced another raft of excellent designs. Of these, **FAIRY**, **FAN** [3557] and **Nightingale** [3562] are deserving of attention. The much sought after **FAIRY** pattern, comes mainly on a high lustre blue ground [3564] or orange [3576], although whispers abound of a fabled yellow ground. Even some eighty years after Best Ware production ceased, a never previously seen colourway or design may appear, to furrow the brow of collectors and experts alike.

FAIRY

The **FAIRY** pattern, as shown on a veined, orange, twin handled pedestal fruit bowl, is a good example of shape, colour and form. The central figure takes its origin from that first seen in the artist's watercolours of 1927, and clearly the pixie-like hat of the fairy is from the same source. The gilt outline of the figure, wings and 'bubble', has been infilled by the pottery in a beguiling luminescent manner. The inclusion of the dramatic shadow was typical of Miss Elmer's decorating technique. **VICTORIAN LADY**, [3451] **DEVIL** [3767] as well as **JACOBEAN FIGURES** [3856] are all blessed with this unique attribute. The trailing strand of floral artwork is set on a lace-like black ground. Overglaze painting of the flowers is minimal but the colour palette and composition are impressive. The overall design is balanced by the inclusion of a small floral section to the foot of the bowl. The gilding to the top rim, foot, as well as the handles, enhance the high glaze lustre finish, a fine free-form example of the art deco movement.

FAN

Miss Elmer's ideas must have been fulfilled by the **FAN** pattern, which was produced on either a ruby or powder blue ground. The ruby version [3558] has a marbled effect, achieved by the skill of the aerographer. However, the blue version [3557] also shows the design to good effect. The rainbow-like fan motif is formed by a combination of lithograph and gilt transfer. Lower down, the pattern comprises three circular roundels. They reflect the orient in much the same way as did the interpretations of the top European jewellers of the day. A brooch on these lines was shown at the 1925 Paris Exhibition. The French jewellers were fascinated by the ceremonial jewellery of India and had dealings with the Maharajahs. The art deco style was reworked into pieces of oriental origin. It is rewarding to study the complexity and detail of the **FAN** pattern. The patience and skill of the Carlton Ware enamellers would have been tested by the onglaze ornamentation. The task was made more onerous by clusters of bubbles, all of which had to be filled by the tip of a sable and squirrel hair brush in a variety of colours. The pieces with their mother of pearl interior, would be completed in the customary manner, with gilding to rim and base. Art Deco is wonderfully represented in products such as these; sunrises, rainbows, lightning flashes and radiant motifs were the stock in trade of the pottery's luxury line at this time. There is an amazing array of minute multi-coloured dots and dashes, which augment these designs. Such prodigious feats of onglaze enamelling can also be seen on patterns such as **BELL, FLOWER AND FALLING LEAF**, **Needlepoint, PERSIAN GARDEN, RIVER FISH Shubunkin and WAGON WHEELS.** As with so many of Miss Elmer's intricate designs, more exquisite elements reveal themselves on each subsequent inspection.

Nightingale

Nightingale [3562] completes the trio of featured designs from 1932. Although the pattern graced several shapes, it was presented in some style on one particular 9" vase. The futuristic tripod feet with matching handles gives the vase a rocket like appearance. Although other ground colours exist, such as blue lustre, the combination of dark green and black is the most effective. The vase is decorated both under and onglaze with spirals of multicoloured flowers and dewdrop leaves in a spectrum of glorious enamels. Two striking bouquets of mixed flower heads are shown on the reverse. Violet was known to have loved flowers and whether in direct interpretation or, as here, in a stylised form, the result was always pleasing. The positioning of the design, the use of space, coupled with the placement of small constellations of colour were prime factors in her art. The eye is unmistakably drawn to the exotic nightingale singing whilst perched on a golden bough. The abundant application of gilt, mother of pearl interior and internal frieze complete the transformation of the product. It is worth recording the ingenious marking of the vase. The central lower point bears the "Carlton Ware" legend and the underside of one of the feet records pattern number 3562 and original order number, O/2895 – which relates sadly to an unknown retailer.

Designs 1933

The dawning of 1933 was accompanied by the first of a host of new designs. It was most likely that this year heralded such notable achievements as **Egyptian Fan,** [3695] **Scimitar**, [3651] together with **Dahlia and Butterfly** [3606]. The gold standard design of **Egyptian Fan** epitomises the prowess of the Copeland Street workforce. Best seen on a stepped vase [777], this brilliant art deco pattern on a ruby marbled ground [3695] conveys all that is best about the firm's luxury products of the day.

Egyptian Fan (front)　　　Velox bowl　　　Egyptian Fan (reverse)

The design was also produced in a variety of body colours on such ware as bowls, ginger jars and candlesticks, the main fan often mirrored on the reverse. The amount and complexity of the raised enamels is commendable. A wonderful array of dashes, dots and circles was applied to the outline of the design by the consummate skill of the enamellers. The fan being stylishly repeated in gilt with a black shadow. The impressive use of black enamel and the attention to border and foot rim is only exceeded by the generous gilding of the main feature. The application is completed by Miss Elmer's tell-tale trees, which boast a veritable cornucopia of hand painted flowers. Patterns, however applied, do not always harmonise with a given shape, but in this case an ideal relationship is formed between the symmetry of the vase and the contours of the design. The same composition is also displayed on the powder blue Velox bowl [3696].

It would be difficult to find a more exuberant art deco design than **Scimitar** [3651] illustrated on an ovoid 456 shape lustre vase. The

Scimitar

jap blue ground with parcel gilt, has gained interest from the array of handpainted coloured dashes. A series of segmented patterns explode in arcs of sunbeams and fire, ceramic pyrotechnics in a geometric frame. Violet is here, in the unique detail, filigree borders and the tracery sublime. The iconic design, furnished with cropped roundels and black and gold panels, speaks of the exciting, decadent times.

Regarding the final example from 1933, **Dahlia and Butterfly** [3606] both the flower and butterfly coloured transfers have been applied to a vibrant handpainted body of black and green. Strong additional colours of blue and magenta outline the main features, with a minimum of gilding used to great effect. Minute touches of top glaze enamel adorn the wings of the butterflies. As can be seen from jug shape 790, the green ground is treated with handpainted underglaze scrolls. This technique was used by Miss Elmer to enhance chosen patterns. As has been seen, such enriching has been found on

Dahlia and Butterfly

Scimitar, WAGON WHEELS [3812] on the green ground, giving a fish scale affect, and on the Handcraft **Geometrica** [3566] depicted in a series of dark blue crescents.

Designs 1934
At this time the pottery was gradually emerging from the doldrums but sufficient interest existed to enable production of the art deco and fantasy pieces to continue. The workforce was certainly put to the test in 1934 by their Oxford mentor in designs such as **BELL**, **DEVIL** [3767] and **Rainbow Fan** [3700]**.** Perhaps of all Miss Elmer's creations, **BELL** is one of the most beautiful and

BELL on ruby (front)

BELL on ruby (reverse)

BELL on lemon

demonstrates admirably the expertise of the unflagging workforce. As was usual, the factory chose to display the **BELL** pattern on a number of colourways, matt green [3786], ruby lustre [3788], and lemon lustre [3774] being prime examples. The patterns are illustrated on a marbled, ruby ground, art deco vase and also on a lemon ground, covered vase. A flower encrusted geometric spectacular is dramatically offset with angulation of the finest detail in blue and green. It is all here in this premium product - the use to perfection of transfers, and under and overglaze work of the finest quality. Marry this to the bijou ornamentation of the bell motif, floral tendrils and border, and you have an outstanding Carlton Ware product. In the study of top glaze enamelling, there surely cannot be a better Wiltshaw and Robinson example than **BELL.** The multiplicity of hand applied colour truly illuminates the design.

The much sought after **DEVIL** [3767] is a derivative of **Devil's Copse** [3787] which is often seen on the powder blue ground. Although accorded the name **DEVIL** by the factory, the additional names of Red Devil or Mephistopheles relate to the same piece. By reference to the objects shown, it can be seen that although the basic elements are alike, the pattern has been applied in a dissimilar way in some areas. Different size transfers have also been used to compensate for the varying size of the ware. The main structural element of the gilt tree supports a canopy of inventive foliage dripping with top enamels and peacock-like eyes. Some of this is repeated in a rich display of seed and flower heads. The concept of a strong, main design, with secondary cameo patterns in a fusion of seemingly incongruous colours, reveals an astonishing result.

In the case of the **DEVIL** pattern itself, the dramatic use of black enamel and under-glaze handpainted shadows are striking features. The prominent figure of Mephistopheles is orange clad within a gilt transfer and the 'fairy-like' shadow affords extra depth to the pattern. The sinuous figure portrays the artist's deftness of touch as originally seen in her water colours.

Devils Copse

DEVIL

Rainbow Fan

Within the same time frame, **Rainbow Fan** [3700] made its entrance - a stylish kaleidoscopic offering. It consisted of a strident, geometric design, on a sponged green ground, featuring a random array of lithographic transfers, some overlapping each other. A rainbow like no other, the reversed fan motif is smothered in fantasy seed heads, tulip shape flowers and butterfly wing insignia. The complete design as seen here, on a 6" vase is a masterly mixture in vibrant under and overglaze polychrome enamels. The theme is continued on the reverse with the design juxtaposed in an inventive manner. Special mention is warranted with regard to the broken border, cleverly conceived and used to great effect with this pattern. The pottery used the same jagged border, but reversed, on **Needlepoint.** As usual, top enamels exist in minute delicacy. The ingenuity of the Copeland Street arts department can be witnessed in these three radically different but vigorous designs.

Designs 1935

Over the next few years, progress would continue in the luxury market and no more so than in 1935 when, in artistic terms, the factory was at its zenith. In that year, Violet conferred her name to **Needlepoint** [3815] on the powder blue ground, **PERSIAN GARDEN** [3893], on the black enamel, and **WAGON WHEELS** [3813] on the sponged pink ground. Her library of design was progressively expanding with well constructed, engaging patterns. The suitably named **Needlepoint** attains an unusual appearance by use of border elements in the main pattern. The grouping of gilt

Needlepoint comport

transfers, overpainted with strong top enamels, is of distinctly modern appearance. The rakish flower and star arrangement is randomly spaced to good effect and makes a refreshingly unfussy concoction which is enriched by the configuration of the splendid broken border.

PERSIAN GARDEN

A powerful expression of Miss Elmer's talent is **PERSIAN GARDEN.** This is a hanging garden of millefleurs and delightful floral minutiae. The bulbous vase shown, again welcomed the inclusion of roundels. Each one bearing a different characteristic synonymous of the colourist's work. The detail of this specimen is delicately executed and perhaps comprises floral blooms, a ribbon of stars, and feather-like leaves. The adjacent pendulous tree arrangement is extremely fine and includes two itinerant border sections and, if viewed carefully, an exquisite small butterfly. Once again the underglaze transfers are adorned by a full repertoire of onglaze enamels. The unusual black lustre ground, combined with the border, frieze and ruby interior, heralds Wiltshaw and Robinson, ably assisted by Violet Elmer, as one of the major quality manufacturers of the day.

WAGON WHEELS was unjustly named by the factory in 1935. A design of such splendour, deserved a less mundane description. The pink ground and border of this geometric pattern demands special attention. It has no less than seven floral circles and stylised stems with attendant foliage, all shadowed in a light blue wash. The pattern is replicated on the reverse, leaving ample space for the enjoyment of

WAGON WHEELS

the wonderful pink ground. Miss Elmer's palette, fed by an expansive compendium of colour was seemingly inexhaustible. Like slices of a dissected lemon or orange or a micro mosaic brooch, the vase is emblazoned with the designer's badge of office. The pattern is well placed on the elegant 8" slimline vase [shape 167], which would be a valued asset in any collection. By virtue of the special onglaze formula, the stylised flowers benefit once again from the painstaking use of the enamellers brush.

Designs 1936

FLOWER AND FALLING LEAF

FLOWER AND FALLING LEAF [3949] and **Lacecap Hydrangea** [3969] arrived in 1936 maintaining the standard of the previous years. The panoply of onglaze enamelling to **FLOWER AND FALLING LEAF** is again outstanding. The large polychrome flower head, inclusive of the outer semi circle, contains several hundred hand-applied dots and dashes. Include the enamelling to the remaining segmented flower heads and border, and an astonishing total of individual applications is revealed. The spectacular raised enamels, displayed on the marbled ruby jug [3949], almost overshadow the other key elements. Underglaze and gilt transfers, interior medallion frieze, together with a delicate green interior are all set off with gold bandings, floral stems and handle.

Lacecap Hydrangea

The highly glazed, two-tone pink and blue ground of **Lacecap Hydrangea** ideally blends with the underglaze transfers on which the floral images are superimposed. The pattern is a success in terms of a good stylistic representation of the flowers of this deciduous shrub. Top enamels, in the time honoured Carlton style, on an interesting montage of colours, add vibrancy to the twin handled vase shown. Gilding has been administered where necessary and the rich ruby interior finished with a medallion frieze.

Designs 1937

The flow of ideas continued in the penultimate year of Violet Elmer's reign. A prime example of the year's work was **Secretary Bird,** an example of which was produced on ruby ground as pattern number 4018. A combination of stylised flowers, as well as a fantasy bird, were used as a vehicle to display the skill of the designer and 'craftsmen'. The common name of 'Road Runner' seems a little unjust. A dazzling array of hand applied pin pricks of colour, combined with micro dots, dashes and flowers, sets the seal on a delightful petite piece of art. The African raptor has been spectacularly enhanced by raised enamels, reminiscent of hand embroidery. The circumference, is adorned by a minute band of woodland flowers. The example shown has an internal pearlised pastel green finish, complete with cobweb frieze. This is mirrored externally on turquoise and cleverly diverts to embrace the bird motif. The final touches of gilding to top and foot rim, along with general application of gilt transfers, render the piece entire. The creator's output was prolific and **Secretary Bird** was certainly a worthy example of her work in 1937.

Secretary Bird

Designs 1938

After a decade of creativity, the modest Miss Elmer was about to sign off with a final design collective. A chapter was coming to a close in the design annals of the Carlton Works. From Horace Wain, by way of Enoch Boulton and Violet Elmer, the responsibility was about to be passed to Irene Pemberton.

Violet Elmer's wonderful work at the factory was coming to an end and she would shortly leave and marry.

Babylon

Some of the prime examples of her work in that final year were patterns known as **Babylon** [4125] and possibly **STAR FLOWER** [4215]. **Babylon** was in the mould of the top level 'no expense spared' Carlton Ware lustre products. The pattern is displayed on a green and yellow, sponged and hand painted body. Bell and star like flowers rival one another in a landscape festooned with tropical foliage. The main focus of the design is a multi-pointed sun, which is filled with a plethora of minute polychrome beads. The whole arrangement is replete with gilt transfer print and attention to rims.

STAR FLOWER

STAR FLOWER [4215] is something of a mystery, as it is officially accredited to Irene Pemberton due to the pattern number. It nevertheless speaks of the in-house factory style, which was heavily influenced by Miss Elmer. Therefore it is a worthy inclusion. The design was usually to be found on ruby lustre ground [4215] or on the much prized matt pale blue ground [4216]. The main floral emblem provides the catalyst for the art deco sprays of fanciful flowers and leaves. The fastidious peripheral decoration is quite masterful. The pattern was printed and painted under glaze, after which it was reprinted in gold with additional raised enamels. The ruby example shown demonstrates the use of a medallion frieze to the top outer rim, thereby leaving the interior unencumbered.

The desk from the factory, complete with paint pots, on which so many of Violet's designs were produced, is reputed to survive.

Miss Elmer's work was finally done, leaving an outstanding legacy for the enjoyment of future generations.

A fine display of Carlton Best Ware

The vexed question as to value of Best Ware, is perhaps better left to those more qualified. It is sufficient to say however, that aided by major auction houses, the strong market peaked about a decade ago. At auction in July 2000, a record price of nearly £10,000 [including charges] was established with the sale of a large **JAZZ** ginger jar. Today's values are considerably less than those achieved in the heady days, nonetheless the collector should expect to pay a premium for an exceptional piece in 'perfect' condition.

Although Best Ware can still be found in traditional auctions, fairs still appear to prosper and a number of specialist dealers still survive, it is the rise of the internet site that has brought about the biggest change.

In a way, the decline of the local antique shop is a sad reflection of the times. Its demise is restrictive and lessens the enjoyment of the undertaking in favour of the 'armchair collector'.

Chapter 16

Marriage and the Changing Times

The 25th June 1938 was to see the Reverend Stather-Hunt officiate at yet another wedding ceremony at St Matthews Church, Grandpont, Oxford, this time involving Miss Violet Irene Ellen Elmer and her beau Arthur Joseph Lawton, b. 12.04.1908 of Stone Road, Lightwood, Longton. [Lightwood Road A5005 is the present day counterpart]. Mr Lawton was a master at the Broadmeadow County Secondary School, Chesterton, Newcastle-under-Lyme where he taught woodwork.

Violet's links to Oxford were strong, the church being but a short distance from her place of birth. Photographic records survive of this memorable day in Violet's life. The following additional information was recorded on the marriage certificate. The bridegrooms father, Alfred, was described as "insurance agent" whilst the bride's father, Thomas Henry, now 72 years of age, as "retired". Witnesses were Violet's brother, Wilfred Henry George and sister Florence Esmé Nicols [Elmer]. Arthur was described as "bachelor/teacher" and Violet simply as "spinster/designer".

After a decade of service, personal circumstances meant the end of her design association with the company. The time worn adage 'cometh the hour, cometh the man' was never more appropriate, as Violet's skills unmistakeably epitomised the flamboyant evocative inter-war period at Copeland Street.

Vast changes were on the horizon with the outbreak of the Second World War looming. A shortage of manpower, materials and markets would severely curtail activities at the Carlton Works.

From 1942 the company was constrained by wartime legislation to the production of utility ware for the home market. Items would have been of a white, undecorated nature or in the case of some floral embossed ware of a 'dumbed down' flat yellow or green appearance. The industry generally suffered in this way. As regards the export market, restrictions were less severe and fully decorated pieces continued to be made throughout the time of the hostilities. It wasn't until a decade later, in August 1952, that the Board of Trade lifted the ban and allowed the sale of decorated ware to the home market.

The environment in which the designer had prospered for so long soon vanished and with it the ethos of liberated artistic expression.

Post war fashion changed and in the immediate period of austerity, ceramic design had, of necessity, become more one dimensional and mundane. Never again would the quality, excess and elegance of the earlier years be matched. Miss Elmer had chosen the time of her departure well.

Violet's Wedding Day

Chapter 17

Products 1939 - 1967

A Broad Overview

Following Miss Elmer's departure, and up to 1967, when the premises were sold to the Wood Group, the products represented the new times. After some years, a shift in style would result, and with hindsight, a more 'retro look' emerged. The production of floral and fruit embossed ware continued, albeit initially under Government restriction, but other lines were developed during and after the War. However, a distinction could sometimes be detected in later techniques. The new ranges which were being rolled out augmented the production of long standing lines. At the beginning of the war, embossed items such as Begonia, Campion, and Narcissi were developed.

Post war, embossed examples being produced included Delphinium, Hydrangea, Poppy and Primula. Available in more than a dozen shapes, Primula was a naturalistic offering in a choice of either green or yellow. Foxglove was another popular design which deserves some elaboration. No doubt designed by Rene Pemberton, it came to prominence in early 1940, with a few shapes to test demand. According to the shape books, the range was soon enlarged to well in excess of a dozen pieces, which could be further differentiated by various sizings. It was produced, in green, yellow or sometimes a pinky-beige colourway. The shape number for each piece is documented. The product was still being advertised in the trade magazines of 1946 and 1948. This affords a contrast to some later lines where only one basic shape was produced, although with colour variations.

1946 Advertisement

In the late 1940s, Poppy, together with Poppy and Daisy were brought to national attention. Examples abound. Hydrangea, just a few years later, was again typical of the period. Excluding differing sizes, seventeen different shapes are recorded in Hydrangea, including a lamp-base, vase, tray, bowl and preserve. The range was offered in either pale green or pale blue. The ground colour would have been applied by the aerographer and then the underglaze paintress would colour the flower petals, stem and leaves by hand, prior to glazing. At this time, the factory named embossed Vine pattern [sometimes known as Grape], was also introduced. Attractive as they were, these later pieces display a lack of subtlety in comparison to the embossed pieces of the 1930s.

Shortly after the Second World War, the Royale range was unveiled. The designs were set off on a ground of bleu, noire, the ever popular rouge, or vert. "Handpainted" was often added to the backstamp. Other products of the time according to trade advertisements, included a range of candle-holders, which incidentally were not unique to this period and crinoline lady cruets. Floral embossed ware continued to be designed, manufactured and flourished well into the 1950s.

The same decade was noteworthy for Carlton Ware's excursion into the production of advertising ware for the brewery and associated trades, leading it to become a major manufacturer in that field. Orders for the Guinness Brewery took centre stage and were fulfilled in large quantities from 1955 until 1963. Well known items such as a set of flying toucans, the zoo collection, as well as lamps featuring a toucan, penguin or a sea lion gained recognition.

Fruit Ware, another new concept was introduced in 1959 and was available until the late 1970s. As the name implies, it consisted of tableware and especially, amusing cruet sets, modelled in the form of carrots, pea pods, apples and pears. At this time there was still a demand for the more traditional, high quality lustre ware. In 1959 the company was advertising a tea service in **SPIDERS WEB** pattern on a light ground. The late 1950s continued to be a busy time at the factory, with Magnolia and Convolvulus best illustrating the new generation of floral embossed ware.

1959 Advertisement

The fashionable new line of 'Windswept' was also conceived at this time. The clean cut design reflected the new movement and was created in response to demand for a modern product. In Britain, Carlton Ware was by no means alone in this development, which belatedly followed the lead given by European and American designers in the immediate post war period. The ware, which was aimed at a specific market, came in three sets of twin tone colours. The simple design, bereft of much decoration, was achieved by aerography, with the pattern added as a transfer. Carlton's 'Pinstripe' followed and was well suited to the times. It was aiming at a similar clientèle. Preserves, egg sets and cheese dishes were prominent in this series, manufactured in a characteristic leaf design, with pronounced veining. Over a hundred years earlier,

Wedgwood had a not dissimilar product. Echoes of the pioneering 'Windswept' could be seen as the 1950s exited in favour of the 1960s.

1961 Advertisement

Starved of decoration, whether from transfer print or mould, the modern tableware appeared utilitarian and stark compared to that produced pre-war. The attitude of the British public had certainly changed with acceptance of these modern products. The Staffordshire pottery industry generally had been compelled to change course, and close rivals like Crown Devon were moving in the same direction with contemporary designs.

The more efficient slip moulding process was used in the construction as opposed to the potter's wheel. At the 'clay end' of the factory, raw materials of clay, stone and flint were used in the process of creating the liquid slip. These were broken down by the blunger, and then electro magnets removed any iron particles. Details of the new pattern, colourway and shape of vase, all of which had been created in the art department, would have been passed to the modelling shop. Present in the 1920s was Bob Mitchell, who, with Ron Hopkinson, worked closely with Miss Elmer, modelling shapes. Bob Mitchell, who left Carlton Ware after the war for better prospects in the film industry, was related to Reginald, the designer of the Spitfire and had connections in the pottery industry. From the model a master mould would be created, from which many additional moulds for working use would follow.

In the casting shops the clay slip would be applied to the moulds; handles, covers and finials were cast separately. Following drying, the first or biscuit firing would take place. After each process the ware would be fired at different temperatures according to the stage of production. Before 1946 Wiltshaw and Robinson's two large bottle ovens would have been in constant use, as well as the nearby muffle oven. The muffle kiln had an inner chamber thus preventing the ceramic from being exposed to extreme temperatures.

After the rough edges of the moulded joints had been fettled, the porous matt body of the vase would soon be ready to receive a ground colour. Aerography, or air brushing, which obviated the need for the earlier more labour intensive method of applying the base coat, was used to blow the colour onto the ware. This method offered more control and flexibility than the previous dipping or hand painting options and enabled glorious marbling effects to be obtained. The revolutionary technique of spray painting was developed in the United States of America during the late 19th century. One of the pioneers, Charles L. Burdick, of Madison, Wisconsin moved to London and in 1893 established the Fountain Brush Company in order to manufacture his air brush and in doing so, created the term 'aerograph'. In 1900 the company changed its name to Aerograph Co. Ltd. to better reflect the product. The new apparatus evolved and as well as the pottery industry, found wider application in the finishing shops of the aircraft industry. Wiltshaw and Robinson soon adopted the new technology, with the result that the aerographers at Copeland Street were now better paid than the paintresses.

The next process was the application of the underglaze decoration by either hand painting or multicoloured lithographic transfer. With regard to transfer printing, the process was initiated by the designer whose drawings would have been passed to the engraver and lithographer to allow reproduction of the pattern onto metal plates. Colour was added by the printing section and the pattern transferred onto special paper, [decals] via the roller press. The tissue containing the required image would then be passed to the next section of the works for trimming and fixing to the vase.

POTTERY MANUFACTURE ~ PAINTING

The following is from a series of articles which appeared in The Pottery Gazette and Glass Trade Review, 1931.

Ornamentation by brush-work is one of the most interesting and intriguing phases of pottery decoration.

Flowers, leaves, dots, lines, etc., are executed by paintresses expressly trained for the purpose, and each girl excels in a particular branch of ornamentation.

Sureness of touch is acquired only by constant practice and repetition. Painting is done both under and over glaze, and affords great liberty of expression, particularly when guiding lines are dispensed with.

When faint outlines are merely filled in by means of brushwork, the process is known in the trade as "enamelling".

The engaging **RIVER FISH Shubunkin**, also clearly demonstrates the use of underglaze hand painting. The portrayal of the seaweed fronds, marine vegetation to the foot of the vase, together with the shadow of the fish, were all applied freehand by the paintress prior to the next stage of the operation. As previously mentioned, the shadow element is a typical Violet Elmer feature and is to be found on several of her other designs. The paintresses had considerable licence to interpret the watery scene, as no two 'fish' vases would be exactly the same. An alchemic understanding was essential, to allow a product to successfully emerge from the kiln in the desired condition. Inevitably from time to time problems did occur. There was for instance, a tendency for the black enamelling of some chargers to oxidize over the years.

The next requirement was the glazing of the vase, which would eliminate porosity and provide a hard strong surface. Not many of the skilled staff who pursued a career at Copeland Street before the last World War, survive. Sadly, recent times have marked the passing of the former head dipper who commenced work at the factory in the early 1930s. Over a lifetime he expertly administered glaze to many thousands of pieces by dipping them into a specially prepared solution. As this was done by hand, such a large scale unhealthy practice would probably be condemned by today's enlightened society. The craftsman met his future wife at the pottery. She worked nearby at the 'clay end' as a 'sponger', and like her husband, devoted most of her working life to the firm.

The stage was now set for the application of lustre, by which means the earthenware item would acquire a wonderful depth of colour. A coat would be applied freehand with a broad brush. Lustre was also applied to the interior to obtain a mother-of-pearl finish. Lustring was an area in which the Copeland Street complex excelled, having developed a superb range of a dozen or more colours over many years. No effort was spared, as is also demonstrated by Carlton's proclivity for the use of delightful colours for internal decoration. Dependant on design, whether a matt or high glazed piece, interiors of black, blue, brown, green, pink or red could be found, glorious enough to deter usage as a flower vase.

The GLAZE puts the finish on your work

Ensure the best results at a reasonable cost by always using RAMSDEN'S GLAZES

VELVET MATT and BRIGHT GLAZES IN ALL SHADES OF COLOUR

LEADLESS GLAZES
IVORINE &
HONEY GLAZES
TILE GLAZES
CHINA GLAZES
LEAD FRITS
BORAX FRITS
ENAMEL COLOURS
UNDERGLAZE
    COLOURS
GLAZE STAINS

ALUMINA
ANTIMONY OXIDE
BALL CLAYS
BARIUM CARBONATE
CADMIUM SULPHIDE

CHROME OXIDE
COBALT OXIDE
COPPER OXIDE
CORNISH STONE
DIAMOND CHINA CLAYS
FELSPAR
FLINT
FLUORSPAR
IRON OXIDE
MANGANESE
RUTILES
SELENIUM
TIN OXIDE
TITANIUM OXIDE
URANIUM OXIDES
WHITING
ZINC OXIDE

ALL OTHER MATERIALS FOR GLASS AND POTTERY

SOLE AGENTS FOR
**LIBREX GLASSMAKERS RED LEAD
LIBREX LEAD BISILICATE
LIBREX WHITE LEAD**
The Best for Pottery and Tile Glazes

LIQUID GOLD and PLATINUM

C. E. Ramsden & Co. Ltd.

Longton 3242 and 3243
Cables: Stoke-on-Trent

GLAZE AND COLOUR MANUFACTURERS AND MILLERS OF ALL POTTERY MATERIAL
FENTON, STOKE-ON-TRENT

There were fundamental differences in the production of **Crested Bird and Water Lily** and the **RIVER FISH Shubunkin** vases. One had an underglaze transfer with a modicum of overglaze enamels, whereas the other had an abundance of overglaze decoration. However, additional procedures to both were necessary. Friezes and borders would be transfer printed in a similar process to that used previously. Overprinting with a gilt transfer in 22 carat gold, to outline the pattern, in order to make provision for an onglaze finish was essential. Following the operation of hand painting to foot and rim and subsequent burnishing, both vases would proceed to the enamellers. With the gilt outline in place, they could now exercise their craft. Both vases would now finally be complete, with in particular, **RIVER FISH Shubunkin**, a leading Violet Elmer pattern providing one of the best examples of the enameller's skill.

Burnishing - Carlton Works c.1952

Although this is a general outline of the main process, there were many variations and other factors involved, both in the manufacture of Best Ware and other products. These included the use of litho transfers [silk screen prints made with 22 carat gold], gilt sheet transfers, the buying in and use of transfers from specialist companies, choice of lustres, decoration by dimpled print, raised paste or jewelling. General processes may have required use of paint in powder form during firing and judgement, particularly in the use of cobalt oxide. Include printing, painting and enamelling, both under and overglaze and the complex nature of the task can be seen. The use of a sponge to obtain a mottled background effect was an additional skill. This technique was applied to the Handcraft jug, **CLEMATIS** [3525], **Rainbow Fan** [3700], **WAGON WHEELS** on pink [3813], and René Pemberton's **Spangled Tree** [4163]. Other issues are also intriguing. Some of the Best Ware products of identical nature were disproportionate in weight, which goes to show what an inexact science potting was. It is also interesting that on some grounds, particularly the blue, some ceramics appear to take on a darker hue depending on the intensity of natural light.

Unglamorous as part of the manufacturing process undoubtedly was, collectors are fortunate today, to be the beneficiaries of such accomplishments.

Handcraft and Best Ware Shapes

PARADISE BIRD AND TREE WITH CLOUD Shape 139

A design is not seen to best advantage unless it is applied to the most suitable ceramic shape, whether it be a vase, jug, bowl or other artefact. For example, the stepped conical art deco vase shape 777 is exploited to greatest advantage by angular geometric patterns rather than those of a floral nature. Vase shape 442 affords an expansive display area and because of its timeless shape, can carry motifs of any type. Some shapes, such as vase 139, are seemingly best suited to more traditional patterns.

A successful marriage enhances the product whereas a mismatch can be cause for regret. In general, the origin of some shapes is lost in antiquity whilst others share a relationship with the products of other potteries. It would not have been easy for a designer working in close collaboration with the modeller to create an original traditional style vase as the parameters were so narrow. Of the many 'Carlton' shapes produced, some of the more commonly found were numbers 217, 406, 442, 443, 456, 457, 464 and 777. The factory also made good use of covered vase shape 244 and 311 and didn't hesitate to produce jugs in shape 496 and 789.

Shapes - top from left:- 217 [Summer Flowers 3926] 406 [Sunflower Geometric 3333] 442, 443, 456, 457, 464 [Hedgerow 3874] 777 [Tendrillon 3858]
Shapes - bottom from left:- 125 [SKETCHING BIRD 3889] 244, 311, 496 [CLEMATIS 3525] 789

The configuration of a few of Carlton Ware's vases, not forgetting ginger jars, was quite similar to some of those produced by Crown Devon, Poole, Radford and Wedgwood [Fairyland]. There were subtle differences between the shape of many of the Staffordshire decorative pieces. Putting aside art pottery and the realm of character jugs by such firms as Burleigh and SylvaC, it is inevitable that the shape of some products from one factory may on occasion resemble those of another. Shapes were rarely named by Wiltshaw and Robinson and only a few such as **AZTEC** [ovoid shaped dish],

Aztec - AZALIA [4140]

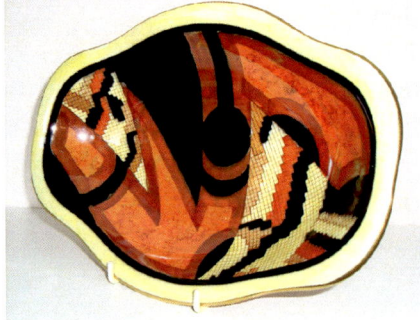

Gondola - Eden [4241]   Revo - Jazz Stitch [3655]

GONDOLA [twin handled footed bowl], **REVO** [dish] and the previously shown **VELOX** [triple-footed bowl] appear to have been accorded this honour. The company's shape books are not overly detailed, a simple description such as 'powder bowl' or 'cigarette box' being deemed sufficient.

Many vases, ginger jars and jugs came in several sizes; reference vases, the classic 406 and conical 777, were both made available in approximate sizes of 6″, 8″ and 10″. Other size options were to be found in covered vase 311 and open vases 442, 443 and 464. The range was complemented by the long established ginger jar shape 125 with the domed cover, which again was available from a selection of different size moulds. The shape numbers indicated, span the period from approximately 1911 [125] to the mid 1930s [789] although precision is difficult.

Borders, Friezes, Finials and Mounts

At this stage it may be appropriate to consider the external borders found on some of the lustre ware. The use of bright enamels gives a vibrant and colourful effect which is far removed from the appearance of internal friezes. Mastery was obtained in furnishing these luxury goods, regardless of cost, with such handsome features. When transfer strips were used, they would have been created, or at least chosen, by say, Miss Elmer as part of her design brief in order to complement the ceramic. Both gilt and lithographic coloured transfers were used, accentuated by pinpricks, strokes and squares of top enamels, prime examples being **BELL, Egyptian Fan**, **PERSIAN GARDEN** and **WAGON WHEELS**. **BELL**, on the ruby ground, is well served by a lace-like black and gold transfer, with the various garlands enlivened by an array of onglaze enamels in many colours. The delicate border matches the design to perfection. The same style of border would be used consistently on a Best Ware piece, but subtle changes of colour to the enamels could be made. The black gilt transfer to the outer rim, or top most extremity of **Egyptian Fan** is finished onglaze in the form of a series of intermittent squares and a number of barely discernible dots. The colours and the symmetry add strength to the art deco design. The **PERSIAN GARDEN** pattern on the black ground is characterised by the geometric banding of the rim with customary enamel treatment. The secondary border, formed by a gilt transfer encompassing small colourful stars, is an unusual and beautifully executed feature which has been added with considerable finesse. Miss Elmer is certainly deserving of praise for devising such an apt adornment to the rim of **WAGON WHEELS,** a delicate gold transfer of swags and segments with top enamels in colours to match the main pattern. A similar border on a larger scale was applied to a green **WAGON WHEELS** jug. The high standard and attention to detail as practised by Carlton Ware has still to receive the recognition it deserves.

Dependent on shape, a large number of Best Ware vases and jugs carried additional decoration in the form of interior, delicate gilt friezes. Handcraft pieces often had a free style painted version, and some patterns, such as **CHINALAND**, a distinctive coloured frieze of their own. Wiltshaw and Robinson were not alone in using this type of decoration, as for example both Fielding's Crown Devon and Wedgwood had their own selection. The general principle seems to be that a vase with straight sides or with a narrowing rim [concave] would not be deemed to benefit from such additional decoration. For example both the '**FAN**' and '**Egyptian Fan**' patterns are treated differently according to shape of vase. Those patterns on concave shape 456 or the stepped shouldered art deco shape 777 do not have additional internal decoration, apart from the mother of pearl finish. It may be that the degree of difficulty in application, or possible detraction from a stand-alone shape, would render an additional border unnecessary. However, the same patterns found on a vase of convex form such as shape

406 include friezes. It therefore seems to be that these ribbon devices are only applied to vases having a flared [convex] rim or a rim with a suspicion of outward movement such as shapes 406, 442 and 457. Where friezes are applied they are consistently matched to the parent pattern, rather than randomly selected. There is considerable duplication owing to the few designs of internal friezes in existence. Size of vase or jug, finish, interior or exterior does not appear to be a consideration. Five different designs are known to have been used on the firm's second generation Best Ware products. As with external borders, it is not known, whether they were named on the works. It is conjecture as to their origin - influences may include the traditional or classical, architectural mouldings, products of other potteries or the friezes may have been simply designed 'in house' at Copeland Street. As an aid to identification the following names have been attributed:

SKETCHING BIRD [border 3891]

Medallion, Lace, Pendant, Cobweb and *Sunrise.* These overprints were not solely used to adorn vase interiors, as the pottery adapted their use in a variety of ways. On **SKETCHING BIRD** [3889] ruby ground and [3891] lemon ground, *Medallion* has been reversed onto a top cover of a ginger jar and applied in more conventional form to the outside rim of a similarly patterned bowl. There are doubtless other examples of such resourcefulness. Although the whole spectrum cannot be surveyed, a limited appraisal of interior friezes reveals that *Medallion* is by far the most popular, featuring on over half the patterns sampled. These include **Devils Copse, FLOWER AND FALLING LEAF**, **Geometric Sunflower** [3333], **JAZZ, Lacecap Hydrangea**, **NEW CHINESE BIRD AND CLOUD** [3322], **PARADISE BIRD AND TREE** [3147], **PERSIAN GARDEN, Summer Flowers** [3926], **TREE AND SWALLOW** [3280], and **WAGON WHEELS**. Although less familiar than *Medallion,* examples of *Lace* can be found encompassing the design of **Crested Bird and Water Lily, Fantasia, FAIRY, Floral Comet,**

Nightingale and **SCROLL**. The seldom seen, *Pendant* can be viewed to good effect on **Hedgerow** [3874] and **RIVER FISH Shubunkin**. Although *Cobweb* and *Sunrise* are quite unique, they are known to be integral features of **Secretary Bird** and the Handcraft, **Geometrica** [3566] respectively. Even with such limited availability it can be seen that pleasing results have been obtained.

clockwise from top left, medallion, lace, pendent, cobweb and sunrise

Dog of Fo - NEW MIKADO

Finials and knops are found on covered vases, ginger jars and powder bowls and used by the designer to complete architectural form. Whether plain or flamboyant, they were moulded separately and affixed to the covers of the appropriate products. Whilst covered vase shape 311 bears a standard finial, the oriental style covers of lidded vases, particularly shape 244, were crowned with a miniature gold turret. Shown on temple jar **NEW MIKADO** [2728] the gilt 'Dog of Fo' is only surpassed by the death mask finial, defiantly

Death Mask Finial - TUT

displayed on a magnificent **TUTANKHAMEN [TUT]** [2711] ginger jar.

Over the years some products included metallic mounts either by necessity or choice. A feature of a number of early bowls was the application of a deep pewter external rim in the art nouveau style. Some Handcraft table lamps were produced, mounted on a metal base. More elaborate examples were made such as the **Secretary Bird** [4017], where a brass base, in the form of acanthus leaves and lion's paw feet, supported the main body. **NEW MIKADO** [rouge royale] was another outstanding example of a lamp with an exotic brass base which on this occasion, comprised diving dolphins. An original lampshade would be of special interest. Amongst other items, biscuit barrels and claret jugs were all engineered with the obligatory silver or silver plate mounts. Wiltshaw and Robinson would have had to buy in these fitments, which presumably were designed by the company, or alternatively the ware could have been sent to the supplier for completion.

Secretary Bird - Lamp Base

NEW MIKADO - Lamp Base

Chapter 19

Tributes and Obituaries

Christopher Boulton 1912-1978
Born 1st October 1912 at Williamson Street, Tunstall, Stoke-on-Trent, John Christopher Granville Boulton was the son of carting contractor Arthur and his Lancastrian wife, Catherine M. Granville. The custom of incorporating the mothers maiden name in that of the children still prevailed. At the time of his birth, a general servant was employed in-house. Christopher Boulton, as he was generally known, was the third of six children. He attended St Mary's R.C. School, Tunstall and Burslem School of Art. Spoken of as a lovely, gentle man, he did not marry and was not related to renowned designer Enoch Boulton. During the war, he served in the RAF as a wireless operator in the Middle East and Italy. Apart from his ceramic career, post war, Christopher became a designer of fabrics at the well known textile company of Wardles at Leek. After a short time there, he returned to work in The Potteries. The designer, who had continued to live at home in Williamson street, Tunstall whilst working in the local ceramic industry, moved to Victoria Street, Cheadle, following retirement. Sadly illness accounted for his untimely death. He died at a family home at Hanley, 18th February 1978, his occupation being listed as "ceramic designer, [retired]".

Christopher Boulton and niece c.1964

Recollections of Rose Colclough 1917 – present

Rose, one of twelve siblings, was born in 1917 and started work at Copeland Street in 1932. She was the only family member to be involved in the industry. The majority of the workforce lived nearby and made their own way to the factory. Although buses were available, the young Miss Colclough walked to work most days from Bucknall, a distance of some five miles each way. This enabled her to save part of her bus fare allowance of two pence per day.

She initially worked with the aerographers, cleaning the ware with a sponge after it had been sprayed. This type of work and the training that followed attracted a day wage. Once trained, the young aerographer would have been paid on a piecework basis. Both biscuit and gloss ware benefited from her skills; once the process was completed, the biscuit ware was fired, then hand painted and fired again. The gloss ware went to painting before it was fired. Rose worked on most things, using all colours especially black, green and yellow. She didn't do ruby ware as this work was carried out by the less capable sprayers as it was easier. Similarly, employees learning the trade would work on rouge ware as the abundance of pattern would cover any spray blemishes. The nozzle of the aerograph was adjusted dependent on which ware was being treated at the time and which effect was required.

The pieces were received on stillages and after completion would be moved on in the same way. This was a difficult single handed manoeuvre with a six foot long loaded board of ware. There were issues concerning the use of lead, which restricted the work of aerographers to a set number of hours per day as imposed by the Health and Safety Act.

Rose remembers working from 8.30am–8pm Monday to Friday and occasionally Saturday mornings, but weekends were not compulsory. However, these times may include a considerable element of overtime, as it should be remembered that employees were all on piecework and wished to maximise the situation.

Paid holidays are also recalled. The official Holidays with Pay Act, was introduced in 1938, guaranteeing industrial workers at least one weeks holiday with pay a year. The company's annual shut down was almost certainly during the first two weeks of August. Popular holiday destinations of the time were Blackpool and Rhyl. Although understandably Rose's memory may have dimmed a little with time, she reveals that paintresses were located by the large windows on the first floor of the main building with a later expansion to the second floor. Staff were allowed to buy seconds, and visits to the showroom [shop] on a Friday and also occasionally a Wednesday, are recalled, especially if a 'one off' design became available. There was a works canteen in a nearby street. This was created by the company after the purchase of nearby vacant houses. The employees partook of the traditional mid morning and afternoon breaks but these were unofficial.

During one occasion, it is understood that the pottery was contracted to make a series of dolls heads. These were a bisque product as the use of colour was restricted during the Second World War. Miss Colclough recounts that they were made in a tin tabernacle of a building in the yard, although on one occasion it was severely damaged by an errant bovine which had broken loose en route to a nearby abattoir and found its way into the premises. A veritable 'bull in a china shop'. Although the hours were long, she recalls that the Copeland Street plant was a happy place in which to work, where friendships were formed, lighter moments enjoyed and where practical jokes were not uncommon.

During the War, Miss Colclough left to work at the Swynnerton ammunition factory near Stone. Colleague and friend Dorothy Faulkner followed a similar path. She joined the works in the early 1930s as a trainee paintress and left in 1943 to drill holes in munition shells at the same wartime establishment. After the hostilities, Dorothy rejoined Carlton Ware and was appointed a 'Missus' before retiring around 1980.

Rose Hampson, now with a family of her own, returned to the Copeland Street Works and with the exception of a short dalliance with George Clews and Co (Ltd) Pot Bank in Tunstall, remained at Carlton Ware until retirement around 1977.

BULL IN A CHINA SHOP!

A Bull never gets a break to-day

Time was when a bull could have a happy half hour in your china shop. But not to-day. Bare shelves meet the bovine gaze—unless his entry coincides with the arrival of your Colclough China quota. Even then he might be pushed aside by stampeding housewives. . . . Well, it's hard to please everybody, but we do share out our limited output with scrupulous care. When the Authorities permit we will lose not one unnecessary hour in producing all the Colclough China you need.

LONGTON — STOKE-ON-TRENT·

Colclough China advertisement from 1945 illustrating the effect of wartime restrictions on the pottery industry.

Olive Kew 1902 – 1991

Olive was born 23rd July 1902 at 59, Carlingford Road, West Tottenham, London; her birth was registered in Edmonton in 1903. Being very ill as a child, she was educated at home by her mother until she was 13. In 1904 the family moved to Northampton and by 1911 was living in the town at Towcester Road. In September 1916, Olive, generally known by the nickname of 'Wink' attended Notre Dame High School where her sister Joan had been educated. She stayed there until 1920, after which time she enrolled as Art Pupil/Teacher at Northampton School of Arts and Crafts. It was here that the young Miss Kew, taught ten hours per week and otherwise studied. It is worth recording that Olive must have been possessed of a pioneering spirit, as in 1925 she had a flight in an aeroplane.

Olive worked at the school for six years, until she had passed all her examinations. In July 1927 she was awarded a free studentship to attend the Royal College of Art, but did not pursue this as it would have imposed a further financial burden on her parents. Instead, she gained a position teaching art and needlework at Highfield College, Bispham, Blackpool, but was not happy there and left in December 1929. Incidentally, a sample of her petit point needlework survives.

Over the next thirty years, Miss Kew found work as a designer in the pottery industry. Amongst her employers were, Wiltshaw and Robinson of Stoke-on-Trent.

For much of her life in Staffordshire, 'Wink' lived with her friend and companion Marion Leonard [b.1899-d.1972]. In 1945 Marion married Thomas Claude Young, a Captain in the Merchant Navy, who died in 1975, outliving his wife by a few years.

Olive continued to live for many years at Westlands, Newcastle-under-Lyme, until returning to Northampton in 1976. Olive Kew, who never married, died at Springfield Nursing Home, Northampton, aged 89, on the 14th March 1991.

Irene Pemberton 1911 – 2008

Irene was born in Tunstall in 1911, one of five children, four girls and a boy, to Thomas Henry Pemberton and Alice née Smith. Both parents were artistic, her father being a professional photographer and amateur painter, her mother a singer with a fine soprano voice and an expert needlewoman. Photography was a thriving business during the first half of the twentieth century and Thomas enjoyed very prosperous times, although inevitably his business suffered when he was called up in the First World War. Irene recalls family life revolving around her father's shop and studio, through which most of those involved with the artistic side of the town passed.

Miss Pemberton's education continued and she began work at Wiltshaw and Robinson's Pottery, Copeland Street, Stoke-on-Trent in 1938.

In 1941, Irene married Harry Griffiths, a policeman and well known local footballer. Being of an old-fashioned nature, he was not happy to have a working wife. Irene, however, continued to work for Carlton Ware but left the pottery in 1942 shortly before the birth of her son John. She returned after the war, but left again in 1949.

After leaving Carlton Ware, she helped her brother Duncan and sister Marjorie with a small family pottery they had set up in Fenton. In 1952 she gave birth to Elizabeth, who was to follow in her mother's creative footsteps. Liz is presently head designer for Missoni, the Italian fashion house.

Later in life, Irene bought a small kiln for use at home and decorated pots that were bought in as blanks from various potteries in the locality, subsequently selling them to small retailers.

Irene was a loving mother and unselfish in all she did. She lost her husband in 1981, after caring for him through a long illness. In 1999 she moved to Somerset to live with her son John. She died at Penlee Nursing Home, Weston-super-Mare on the 20th April 2008 at the age of ninety six. Thankfully, her work survives in the many items of Carlton Ware that are much admired today.

New shapes with traditional quality—these are the selling points of the several lines now being produced at the Carlton Works—the home of originality and enterprise.

1937

AGENTS:
London: Mr. S. Prior, 9, Charterhouse Street, E.C.1.   *New Zealand*: Messrs. Aubrey Gualter & Co., P.O. Box No. 625, Wellington, C.1.   *South Africa*: Mr. A. C. McIntosh, P.O. Box No. 3081, Johannesburg.   *Belgium*: Messrs. Ernest Frissen et Fils, 4/6, Rue D'Anderlecht, Brussels.   *Australia*: Messrs. F. R. Barlow & Sons (Pty.) Ltd., Commerce House, 328, Flinders Street, Melbourne, C.1.   *Canada*: Messrs. Oakley Jackson & Farewell Ltd., No. 2, Leader Lane (at 32, Wellington Street, E.), Toronto, 2.

WILTSHAW & ROBINSON LTD., Carlton Works, Stoke-on-Trent.

Chapter 20

Mrs Violet Lawton

Following marriage, it seems that Violet and her husband moved immediately into a recently built property at Beresford Crescent, Westlands, Newcastle-under-Lyme which remained their home for the rest of their lives. It appears that at this stage Violet's professional design career had come to an end and she settled into traditional domestic life. Perhaps modesty, the need for change or even unknown circumstances accounted for Violet's possible reluctance to revisit those earlier halcyon days. Her work was done.

Beresford Crescent, Westlands

It is known that for personal satisfaction Violet did use her skills to thematically decorate the interior of their home, believed to be an art house although evidence no longer exists. Factor in Arthur's cabinet making skills, and the result must have been a very fashionable dwelling.

The remaining fifty years of her life seem rather uneventful when compared to those previous. Violet, who incidentally was proud of her Oxfordshire accent, together with her husband, enjoyed socialising and they were part of a close-knit group of about a dozen friends. Mr and Mrs Lawton were held in high regard within the community. They had a love of children although no family of their own. Apparently numerous outings, Christmas events, parties as well as organised firework displays were held for 'adopted' nieces and nephews. The outgoing couple were affectionately known to the children as 'Uncle Arthur' and 'Auntie Vi'. Mrs Lawton involved herself with charity work as well as other pursuits. They were both active members of the local rambling club from the late 1930s to the late 1960s as well as having a non-participating interest in the neighbourhood drama group.

Loughborough College c.1959 Violet second right

Longsdon Stoke-on-Trent c.1970 Arthur first right. Violet third left

Longsdon c.1985 Friends Wedding Celebration. Violet standing second left.

Violet is known to have cherished her lovely garden. Her long established interest in nature and flora had manifested itself so well as the essential ingredient in her design career.

Life continued until, after many years together, Arthur died in the autumn of 1978. With the support of family and friends Violet lived another decade until her own demise on 8th March 1988. It is

Book of Remembrance

Bradwell

perhaps ironic that having attended the funeral of her lifetime friend, Ruby Russell who pre-deceased her, Oxford 27th February 1988, Violet herself passed away a few days later. Her final resting place is to be found at Bradwell Crematorium, Newcastle-under-Lyme, where she is recorded in the Book of Remembrance. The closeness of their arrival seemed destined to be mirrored in departure. Violet and Ruby, were revealed as far from ordinary. Although Miss Elmer seized her opportunity and left home, she would not forget her childhood friend.

Their life's work complete, celebrate Grandpont, the joy and achievement of your daughters.

Appendices

Appendix a

Some Prominent Best Ware and Handcraft Designs by Violet Elmer

Pattern Name	No.	Date	Pattern Name	No.	Date
BUTTERFLY	3290 H	1929	BELL [lemon]	3774	1934
HAREBELL	3294 H	"	DEVIL [wedgwood blue]	3767	"
ZIG ZAG [beige]	3299 H	"	Devil's Copse [powder blue]	3787	"
			GUM FLOWER	3789	"
Lightning [blue]	3356 H	1930	PRIMULA [mauve]	3745 H[?]	"
Fantasia [pale blue]	3388	"	Rainbow Fan [green]	3700	"
Floral Comet [green]	3387	"			
Sunflower Geometric	3333	"			
			AUTUMN DAISY	3802	1935
Awakening [green]	3453	1931	GARDEN GATE	3863	"
Explosion [blue]	3447	"	Hedgerow [grey]	3874	"
Holly	3418 H	"	HOLLYHOCKS [green]	3818	"
SCROLL [blue]	3411 H	"	JACOBEAN FIGURES [blue]	3856	"
VICTORIAN LADY	3451	"	MODERN CROCUS	3803	"
			Needlepoint [powder blue]	3815	"
			PERSIAN GARDEN [black]	3893	"
CLEMATIS	3525 H	1932	SKETCHING BIRD [lemon]	3891	"
Crested Bird & Water Lily [ruby]	3530	"	Tendrillon	3858	"
FAIRY [orange]	3576	"	WAGON WHEELS [green]	3812	"
FAN [powder blue]	3557	"			
Geometrica	3566 H	"			
Hiawatha	3589 H	"	FLOWER & FALLING LEAF [ruby]	3949	1936
Medley	3587	"	Lacecap Hydrangea [pink]	3969	"
Nightingale [green/black]	3562	"	PERSIAN ROSE [beige]	3975	"
Rosetta	3505	"	RIVER FISH	3970	"
			RIVER FISH Shubunkin	3971	"
ANEMONE	3694 H	1933			
Chevrons [green]	3657 H	"			
Dahlia & Butterfly	3606	"			
DAISY	3693	"	Secretary Bird [ruby]	4018	1937
Egyptian Fan [ruby]	3695	"	Tyrolean Bands	4076	"
Intersections	3690 H	"			
Mandarins Chatting [black]	3653	"			
Mandarin Tree	3672	"			
Scimitar [jap blue]	3651	"	Babylon [green]	4125	1938
Summer Medley	3663 H	"	HAREBELLS [Campanula]	4154	"

Note:
A number of different colourways exist, each with its own pattern number
'H'– after the pattern number denotes a Handcraft design
Factory names are given in 'upper case'
The table shows examples in both a lustre and matt finish

Appendix b

Designers associated with Carlton Ware

Date Circa	Designer	Status where known	Products where known
1912	HASSALL John NB. also cartoonist & poster designer	-	Articulated comical figures
1911 - 1921	WAIN Horace	In house	Chinoiserie, Armand etc
1922 - 1929	BOULTON Enoch	In house	Chinoiserie, Handcraft, Best Ware
1928 - 1938	ELMER Violet	In house	Carlton China, Floral Embossed, Handcraft, Best Ware
1930 - 1931	KEW Olive	In house	Best Ware
1935 – 1938	WILTSHAW Betty	In house	Fruit embossed & tea ware [Redcurrant & Rayure/Moderne]
1938 - 1942 1947 - 1949	PEMBERTON Irene	In house	Floral Embossed, Best Ware
1952 -1954	BOULTON Christopher	In house	(?) Best Ware, floral embossed
1950s	FORSTER Philip	-	Tableware and New Wave products
1950s	BLACKMORE James	-	Guinness Ware
1955 - 1963	GILROY John	-	Guinness Ware [Toucans etc]
1967	FOX Angela	In house	Hovis range
1970s	BRENNAN Vivienne [Ex Wood Group]	-	Money banks
1975 - 1986	MICHELL Roger and NAPIORKOWSKA Danka NB.also artists decorators and potters	Independent	Walking ware, Circus and RJS Range
1975 - 1984	GREEVES Pamela [née Souch]	In house	Money banks, flow blue, Alice Ware
1980s	CRITTENDEN John	-	Rumbelows Money Box
1984 - 1986	GOODING Malcolm	Freelance	Comical Novelty Ware [sheep]
1984 - 1996	FLUCK Peter and LAW Roger NB. also artist, ceramicist and illustrator, cartoonist respectively	Independent	Spitting Image figures

Note: At the time Glacielle Ware was introduced in 1937, there was an unsubstantiated link to a French designer

Modellers

Date Circa	Modeller	Status where known	Known Products
1928 -1945	MITCHELL Bob	In house	Embossed, Best Ware
1930s	NIXON E S	In house	Canadian Confederation Jug
1930s	PARSONS Kathleen	In house	Coronation Figures
1930s [mid]	HOPKINSON Ronald	In house	Embossed, Best Ware
1950s	COXON Ken	In house	Fruit range, novelty cruets

Note: 1920s-1930s WATT Elizabeth Mary [1885 – 1954]
One of a number of independent designers known to have painted Carlton Ware blanks

Note: This does not claim in any way to be a definitive listing and the authors regret any errors that may have occurred. However, corrections and additions will be welcomed via the publisher.

Appendix c

The Works – Personnel
Known Employees pre - 1939

	EMPLOYEE	TRADE	DATE EMPLOYED	PERSONAL DATA
1	AUSTIN F	-	1918	-
2	BARDELL H	-	1918	-
3	BARDELL Harry	-	1918	-
4	BARKER A J	-	1918	-
5	BARKER George	Sales Manager	1918 – 1929	-
6	BICKERTON J	-	1918	-
7	BOULTON Enoch	Designer	1922 -1929	1885 - 1972
8	BOULTON J	-	1918	-
9	BOWERS Amy	Aerographer	-	-
10	BRADSHAW Jess	Head Dipper	1932 - 1987	1916 - 2008
11	BRADSHAW Lily	Sponger	1931 - 1977	1916 - 2001
12	BROAD Miss	-	1918	-
13	BURKES Florrie	Aerographer	-	-
14	BURROUGHS F	-	1918	-
15	CLEWLOW Ted	Printer	-	-
16	COOMER Mrs [Ma]	Glost Warehouse Manager	NB. oldest employee in 1938	-
17	CORNES Betty [née Wiltshaw]	Designer/paintress	1938	1917 - Present
18	DAVENPORT J	Office	1918	-
19	DAVIS Harry	Northern Representative	1938	-
20	DEAN Miss	Office	1918	-
21	EARDLEY C	[?Clay Manager after Sam Pope]	1918	-
22	ELMER Violet	Designer	1928 - 1938	1907 - 1988
23	FAULKNER Dorothy	Paintress/Missus	1931 - 1977	1917 - 2004
24	HAMPSON Rose née Colclough	Aerographer	1932 - 1977	1917 - Present
25	HARRISON Miss	Office	1918	-
26	HEATH Lily	Clay Manageress	1935 - 1989	1921 - 2011
27	HEATH W	Painter	1912	-
28	HOPKINSON Ronald	Modeller	1920s	-
29	KEW Olive	Designer	1930 - 1931	1902 - 1991
30	LEADBEATER May	Aerographer	-	-
31	LEES Albert	Finance Director	1930	-
32	LEIGH Miss	-	1918	-
33	MAITLAND Mrs	-	1918	-
34	MAITLAND W	-	1918	-
35	MITCHELL Bob	Modeller	1920s	-
36	MORGAN W	-	1918	-

Appendix c

The Works – Personnel
Known Employees pre - 1939

	Employee	Trade	Date employed	Personal Data
37	NIXON Stanley	General Manager [Decorating]	-	-
38	PEDLEY W	-	1918	-
39	PEMBERTON Irene	Designer	1938 - 1949	1911 - 2008
40	POOLE May née HODGKINSON	Aerographer	-	-
41	POPE Sam	Clay Manager	1918	-
42	POYNTON Reg	Salesman – Scotland, Ireland and North of England	1930s - 1970s	-
43	PRICE W	-	1918	-
44	PURSER W G [Bill]	Finance Director/Company Secretary	1931 – 1969	-
45	PYE F	Painter	1912	-
46	ROBINSON Harold Taylor	Partner	c.1900 – 1911	1877 - 1953
47	ROBINSON James Alcock	Partner	1890 – 1911	1852 - 1931
48	ROBINSON William Henry	Partner	1890 – c.1900	1854 - 1923
49	RUSHTON S	-	1918	-
50	SMITH L O	[A Manager]	1930	-
51	STANLEY Florrie	Aerographer	-	-
52	STEVENSON Miss	Office	1918	-
53	STREET H	-	1918	-
54	STREET J	-	1918	-
55	TAYLOR Dolly	Aerographer	-	-
56	TUNSTALL E	-	1918	-
57	VYSE J	-	1918	-
58	WAIN Horace	Designer	1911 – c.1921	1886 - 1967
59	WALKER Mrs	-	1918	-
60	WILSON F	-	1918	-
61	WILTSHAW B [Betty]	Designer/Assistant	1935 – 1938	1917 - 2011
62	WILTSHAW D E [Douglas]	Director	1920s - 1960	1902 - 1960
63	WILTSHAW F C [Cuthbert]	Partner/Managing Director	1918 - 1966	1892 - 1966
64	WILTSHAW J F	Partner/Managing Director	1890 – 1918	1861 - 1918

Note: With the exception of the details shown, as yet, no further information is known.

Appendix d

The Works – Personnel
Additional Employees 1939 – 1967
Note: see also Supplementary list 1960

	EMPLOYEE	TRADE	DATE EMPLOYED	PERSONAL DATA
1	BADDELY Joan	-	1941 - 1943	-
2	BAMFORD John	Manager	1966 - 1967	1920 - 2009
3	BARKER Ann	-	-	-
4	BEARDSMOORE Agnes	-	-	-
5	BECKETT A	-	1966	-
6	BECKETT H	-	1966	-
7	BENNETT Gladys [sisters]	Gold Printer and raised enameller	1953	-
8	BENNETT Rachael [sisters]	Paintress	1950 - 1989	1935 - 2008
9	BLOOR [Mrs]	Aerographer/paintress	-	-
10	BOULTON Christopher	Designer	1952 – 1954	1912 - 1978
11	BRADBURY F	-	1966	-
12	BROWNLOW Mrs	Decorating Department	1941 – 1943	-
13	BROWNLOW Rita	-	1941 - 1943	-
14	BUCKLEY Joyce	Order Clerk	Post War	-1990
15	BUNN Marjorie	Paintress	1950	-
16	BUXTON Lily	Aerographer	Post War	-
17	COE K	-	1966	-
18	COPE F	-	1966	-
19	COXON Ken	Modeller	1950s	-
20	DOBSON Linda	Warehouse Manageress	-	- present
21	EVANS Kathleen	Aerographer	Post War	-
22	FENTON R	-	1966	-
23	FERNYHOUGH Joyce	Paintress/Aerographer	-	- present
24	HAYNES Margaret	-	-	-
25	HILL Lily	[Clay End]	-	-
26	JACKSON Arthur	Sales Manager/Sales Director	1954 – 1981	-
27	JOHNSON Ken	Salesman [North]	-	-
28	JONES Ethel	Paintress	1960	-
29	KEELINGS Dorothy	Paintress/Missus	Post War	-
30	KELLY John	-	-	-
31	LEES G	-	1966	-
32	MOULD Marion	Rouge Overlooker	-	-
33	MULLARD Paul	Sales	1960	-
34	OVERHAND Anne	Paintress	1950	-
35	OWENS Tom	Works Manager	1965	-1965
36	RAYNOR Connie	-	-	-

Appendix d

The Works – Personnel
Additional Employees 1939 – 1967
Note: see also Supplementary list 1960

	EMPLOYEE	TRADE	DATE EMPLOYED	PERSONAL DATA
37	RICHARDSON Mavis	Paintress	1949	-
38	ROWLAND Edna	Enameller	1941 - 1943	1927 – 2011
39	SCARRAT Lily	Aerographer	-	-
40	SHAW W	-	1966	-
41	SILKS Lucy	Aerographer	Post War	-
42	SILLITO Mary	-	-	-
43	SPARKES Betty	Aerographer	Post War	-
44	STOKES Mrs	Aerographer	1941 – 1943	-
45	TILL Mrs	Missus	-	-
46	WARD L	-	1966	-
47	WESTON Gertie	Aerographer	-	-
48	WHITEHURST Sheila	-	-	-
49	WHITE C	-	1966	-
50	WILDIG MRS	-	-	-
51	WRIGHT Lily	Glost Warehouse Manager	-	-

Note: With the exception of the detail shown, as yet, no further information is known

Appendix e

With acknowledgement to Keith Martin, a supplementary list of 185 employees from 1960. This was compiled by the late Jess Bradshaw, who, for many years, was the head dipper and union representative at the Pottery. It is likely that the personnel shown have been grouped in departments to the exclusion of office staff. Some names will be familiar when compared to the details of the foregoing periods.

Page 1

J Bradshaw	K. Mulliga
J. Loxon	E Proctor
H. Ellis	M. Faulkner
Cooper	E Bonehill
H. Evans	A Russell
E Jones	V. Rowe
P. Woolley	S. Walsh
J Ball	J Millington
J Hobson	M Haynes
P. Stanford	H. Thomason
E Meigh	P. Boote
Stubbs	H. Hulme
W Harrison	J Jones
E Clowes	R. Watt
Nyatt	O Hargreaves
B Norris	J Phillips
Pelwof	P Nixon
Holding	E Old
L Wright	J Bailey
N. Smith	L. Ruelton
Pritchard	H Bird

Page 2

G. Stubbs	R.E. Bennett
G. Birch	F. Bennett
P. Orkthorne	M. Hawkins
E. Parkes	M. Bunn
F. Whitehurst	S. Whitehurst
W. Arrowsmith	10. Fox
E. Ash	D. Conway
. Smith	G. Briggs
E. Taylor	P. Clay
J. Munslow	V. Murphy
D. Dick	M. Peach
H. Seabridge	P. Lowery
E. Beresford	F.R. Myatt
N. Bailey	N. Orme
E. Painer	T. Turnock
W.J. Bloor	A. Kelly
M.E. Astbury	S. Neale
A. Davis	K. Day
B. Clarke	D. Jones
G. Jones	J. Higginson
W.H. Rigby	M. Bridgeford

PAGE 3

J. Taylor	E. Frost
D. Coxon	R. Key
E. Howe	V. Stacey
H. Harvey	E. Toft
R. Hollins	M. Ledbury
R. Box	M. Cope
E. Cook	N. Sandham
S. Goodwin	J. Bradshaw
E. Spender	M. Shirley
A. Oakes	E. Peter
P. Kelly	L. Blandford
D. Wright	A. Bould
N. Williams	T. Orme
G. Woolrich	R. Jones
A. Stevenson	R. Barkley
L. Robinson	F. Eardley
E. Cope	E. Bridgwood
W. J. Peacock	E. M. Hancock
D. Churchill	E. Bauer
D. Rought-aff	E. Emery
M. Donnell	L. M. Croggett

PAGE 4

J. Perry	J Bradbury
E Barkley	S heyan
J Hissey	JH Alcock
E Espley	Mr. R. Elinor
Alcock	Mrs D Foxall
Heath	Mrs L Bradshaw
JMP arkus	Mrs SO M. Guire
Mr Cosden	Mrs L Chell
I.D. Stubbs	Mrs E Robinson
J Lovatt	Mrs a rielly
J Ward	E Capewell
	A Leaf
R Birch	E Appleyard
D Davies	Mrs Hill
B Martin	Mrs A Turner
F Roberts	Mrs A. Whittingham
Crlome	L. Mountford
Hargreaves	V. Rooter
R Gooden	E. Maitland
R Birch	B. Smith
Wadly	H Cooke

Selected Bibliography

Art Deco Ceramics in Britain - Andrew Casey - published by Antique Collectors Club Ltd. UK - 2008

British Art Deco Ceramics - Colin Mawston - Schiffer Publishing Ltd. USA - 2000

British Pottery Manufacturers 1900 - 2010 - Michael Perry - Ocean Publishing. Australia - 2010

Carlton Ware - The Complete Guide - Dr Czes & Yvonne Kosniowski - CKYK Publishing UK - 2010

Collecting Art Deco Ceramics - Howard and Pat Watson - published by Kevin Francis - UK - 1993

Collecting Guides - Art Deco - Judith Miller - First published in Gt Britain by Dorling Kindersley Ltd. - 2005

Collecting Carlton Ware - published by Francis Joseph UK
	First Impression - 1994
	Second Edition - David Serpell - 1999
	Third Edition	- David Serpell - 2004

Crown Devon - The History of S. Fielding & Co. - Susan Hill - Jazz Publications UK - 1993

Harold Holdway - 20th. Century Ceramic Designer - R Holdway & H Holdway - Landmark Publishing Ltd. UK - 2006

The Vine Pottery, Birks Rawlins & Co - Peter S Goodfellow - published by Antique Collectors Club Ltd. UK - 2006

Catalogues, periodicals and club related publications

An Illustrated Guide to Carlton China - Arthur Puffett

"Carlton Ware" Handbook - Ken Andrew - self published UK - 1992

Carlton Ware Newsletters - Ian Harwood & Jerome Wilson. Nos. 1 - 58. 2002 - present. Canada

Specialist Carlton Ware Sales - Christie's Auction Catalogues UK - 1992 - 2003

The Carlton Times 1993 - 2001

The Carlton Comet 2004 - 2007

The Pottery Gazette and Glass Trade Review [varia]

Index

Aberystwyth, 11
Aerograph Co. Ltd., 131, 132
America [USA], 53, 125, 131
Andersen Hans Christian, 75
Arcadian China - see Arkinstall & Sons Ltd.
Arkinstall & Sons Ltd. [Arcadian China], 26
Ashworth & Bros. [Masons Ironstone], 26
Australian Design, 81
Aynsley J. and Sons Ltd., 69

Badingham - See preface
Bakst Leon, 104
Baltimore China Works, 25
Bamford John, 127
Barker George, 57
Barlaston [Stoke-on-Trent], 21, 30
Barlow F.R. & Sons, 41
Bauhaus School, 59
Belleek Pottery Works Co. Ltd., 81
Berkshire China Ltd., 24
Beswick J. Ltd., 81
Beverley Tableware Ltd., 128
Birks Rawlins [Savoy China/Vine Pottery], 21,63-70,
Birmingham, 24,30
Blackpool, 97,145,147
Blank Edward, 24
Boughey & Wiltshaw, 27
Boulton Christopher [John], 101,102,143
Boulton Enoch, 21,55-59,71,73,75,76,79,87,92,105,118,143
Brain E. & Co. Ltd., [Foley China], 69
Brentleigh Ware – see Howard Pottery Co.
British Expeditionary Force, 2
British Industries Fair, 42,64
Bucknall [Stoke-on-Trent], 144
Burgess & Leigh Ltd., [Burleigh Ware], 66, 137
Burleigh Ware – see Burgess & Leigh Ltd.
Burley & Company [USA], 27
Burslem, 19,20,32,46,78
Burslem School of Art, 17,55,99,143

Carder F.W. 21
Carlton China, 63-70,73,78,86,87,89
Carlton & Kent, 24
Carlton Ware, 17,22-25,33,34,40,42,46-49,53,55,59,71,72,75,78-81,89-91,95,96,100-103,108,109,112,124,125,128,131,133,137-139,145,148
Carlton Works Copeland Street, 17,19-21,24,25,30,33-51,54,55-57,69,75,79,81,83-92,95,101,102,107-118,121,124,130-133,140,144-146
Carnarvon Lord, 56
Carter Howard, 56
Carter Truda, 88
Cauldon Potteries Ltd., 26,27
Cheadle, 143
Chelsea Pottery, 81
Clarke Harry, 75
Clews & Co., 146
Cliff Clarice, 1,66,71
Coalport China Co., 26,102

Colclough Rose, 144-146
Constable John, 3
Cooper Susie, 1 ,72
Copeland W. T. & Sons Ltd. [Spode], 40,46,102
Cornes Betty – see Betty Wiltshaw
County Potteries PLC., 24,25
Cowes, 11
Crewe, 21
Crown Devon – see Fielding & Co. Ltd.

Dashwood Sir Henry Bt., 4-6
Davenport Pottery Co.Ltd., 22
de Morgan William, 40
Derby, 20,33
Diaghilev Serge, 59
Diggle Edith – see Edith Wiltshaw
Dorchester [Oxon], 3
Dressler Conrad, 40
Dulac Edmund, 14
Duns Tew, 4-6

Elizabethan Fine Bone China Ltd., 24
Elmer family, 2-7,31,121
Elmer Violet, 1,2, 6-8, 11-17,21,28,36,41,43,48,51,54,59,64,66,69-73,75-95,97,99,103-105,107-111,113-119,121-123,131,133,135,138,139,151-155
"Estoril" Barlaston [Stoke-on-Trent], 30

Faulkner Dorothy, 145
Fenton, 24,78,148
Fielding & Co. Ltd.[Crown Devon], 25,57,75,81,105,126,137,139
Foley China – see E. Brain & Co. Ltd
Forsbrook, 32
Forsyth Gordon, 17

Goddard John Vivian, 26
Goddard Lee James, 24
Goss W.H., 26
Grandpont – see Oxford
Gray A.E. & Co. Ltd., 72,87
Griffiths Irene – see Irene Pemberton
Grimwades Ltd., [Royal Winton], 55,81,87,128

Haggar Reginald, 17
Hampson Rose – see Rose Colclough
Hanley, 41,44,55,78,143
Harley-Jones A.G. & Co. [Wilton Ware], 52
Hibbert & Boughey, 27
Holdway Harold, 102
Hopkinson Ronald, 131
Howard Pottery Co. [Brentleigh Ware], 96, 128

Icanho, 4
Ipswich, 5,17,55,60,61

Jackson Arthur, 24

Kensington Pottery Ltd., 2
Kent James Ltd., 24
Kew Olive, 21,80,95,147

Kidlington, 6
Kirkhams Ltd., 96
Kirtlington, 5,6

Lawton Mrs – see Violet Elmer
Leek, 102,143
London, 41,147
Longport [Stoke-on-Trent], 22
Longton, 25,27,78
Longton Hall Pottery, 81
Longton New Art Pottery Co., 127
Loughborough, 152
Lustre [lustrine ware], 56

Macclesfield, 21,22,30
MacIntyre James & Co. Ltd., 19
Maling C.T. & Sons Ltd., 66
Masons Ironstone China Ltd. - see Ashworth & Bros.
Medmenham Pottery, 40
Milford [Staffs], 29
Minton Ltd., 17
Mitchell Bob, 131
Morris William, 40
Moss Ruby – see Ruby Russell
Mucklestone, 33
Murray Keith, 82

Newcastle-under-Lyme [including Wolstanton], 19,20,22,28,30-33,36,63,77-80,85,121,147,151,154
[New] Pearl Pottery Ltd., 87
Nixon Stanley, 38
Northampton, 147

Old Foley Pottery, 24
Owens Tom, 127
Oxford [including Grandpont], 1,2,6-8,11,17,77,85,88,107,111,121,154
Oxfordshire, 3-6,151

'Paris Exhibition', 57,59,108
Pemberton Irene, 17,21,81,84,92,99-101,118,123,136,148
Poole Pottery Ltd., 71,87,88,137
Portsmouth 32
Price Brothers Ltd., 22,102
Price Waterhouse, 24
Purser W.G., 22,23

Rackham Arthur, 14
Radford Ltd., 137
Rhead Charlotte, 1
Rhyl, 145
Robinson Arthur, 32
Robinson Harold Taylor, 20,26,27,32,33
Robinson Hubert 26,32
Robinson James Alcock, 20,25,26,31,32
Robinson J.A. & Sons Ltd., 26
Robinson William Henry, 20,25,31,32
Robinson & Beresford, 26
Robinson & Leadbetter, 26
Rollinson Kenneth, 23
Rowley Estate [Tendring Hall], 5

Royal Aero Club, 29
Royal College of Art, 17,147
Royal Crown Derby Porcelain Co. Ltd., 26
Royal Doulton & Co. Ltd., 40,66
Royal Flying Corps., 21
Royal Staffordshire – see A.J. Wilkinson
Royal Venton – see Steventon & Sons Ltd.
Royal Winton – see Grimwades
Royal Worcester Porcelain Co. Ltd., 26
Russell Ruby 11,14,69,85,86,107,154

Sanders Sydney, 27
Savoy China – see Birks Rawlins
Shaw & Copestake [SylvaC], 96,137
Shelley Potteries Ltd., 66,69
Shelton [Stoke-on-Trent], 44
Sheringham, 11
Shorter & Son Ltd., 81
Slater Eric, 69
Smith L.O., 95
Spode – see Copeland & Sons Ltd.
Stafford, 30
Steventon J. & Sons Ltd., [Royal Venton], 66
Stoke-by-Nayland 3-5
Stoke-on-Trent, 17,20,21,27,29,30,32,33,36,44-46,54,57,77-79,81,96,152
Stoke-on-Trent School of Art, 17
Stoke-upon-Trent, 25,28,36,77,78
Stone, 19,20,21,33,145
SylvaC – see Shaw & Copestake

Tendring Hall – see Rowley Estate
Tittensor, 29
Trent [River], 36
Trentham [Stoke-on-Trent], 20,30
Tunstall, 78,143,148
Turner & Wood, 34

Unicorn Pottery Ltd., 22

Valuation, 120
Vine Pottery – see Birks Rawlins

Wade Heath & Co. Ltd., 127
Wain Horace, 51,52,55,118
Wain H.A. & Sons Ltd., 52
Wallingford, 3
Warborough, 3
Wardle & Davenport, 143
Waylen Betty – see Betty Wiltshaw
Wedgwood & Sons Ltd., 40,47,81,82,126,137,139
Weston-super-Mare, 149
Wherstead Park, 5
Whieldon Thomas, 80
Wilkinson A.J. [Royal Staffordshire], 24,71
Wilton Ware – see Harley-Jones
Wiltshaw Alice, 22,30,41
Wiltshaw Betty, 41
Wiltshaw Douglas, 21,23,30,37,63
Wiltshaw Edith, 22
Wiltshaw F.C. [Cuthbert], 17,21,22,25,28-31,37,41,43,55,63,99
Wiltshaw J.F. [James], 19-21,27,33,36,51

171

Wiltshaw & Robinson, 17,19,20,23,25,26, 33,34,38,41-44,50-52,57,63,64,69,75,79, 83,84,86,88,89,91,102,112,115,127,129, 131,132,137,139,142,147,148
Wiltshaw Robinson & Son, 20
Wiltshaw Samuel, 27
Wolstanton – see Newcastle-under-Lyme
Wood Group, 22,24,123,127
Woodstock, 6